IRISH WOMEN WRITERS: TEXTS AND CONTEXTS

Series editors: Kathryn Laing and Sinéad Mooney

Kathryn Laing (ed.), *Hannah Lynch's Irish Girl Rebels:* 'A Girl Revolutionist' *and* 'Marjory Maurice'
Elke d'Hoker (ed.), *Ethel Colburn Mayne: Selected Stories*
James H. Murphy (ed.), *Rosa Mulholland, Feminist, Victorian, Catholic and Patriot*

Advisory Board:
Heidi Hansson, Margaret Kelleher, Gerardine Meaney, James H. Murphy

Advance acclaim

'Elke D'hoker's *Ethel Colburn Mayne: Selected Stories* brings to light a sample of work by an unjustly neglected writer, recovering a selection of texts that have been long out of print. The book is purposefully structured, charting the changing shape of a writer's work in the form of the short story. This is a text to relish: the choice of stories is prudent and generous, and D'hoker's introductory essay is thoughtful and considered. An exemplary instance of recovery, which will assist in the reclamation of a writer of real significance.'
– **Paul Delaney**, author of *Seán O'Faoláin: Literature, Inheritance and the 1930s* and co-editor of *The Edinburgh Companion to the Short Story in English*.

Ethel Colburn Mayne:
Selected Stories

The editor

ELKE D'HOKER is professor of English Literature at the University of Leuven, and co-director of the Leuven Centre for Irish Studies and of the modern literature research group, MDRN. She has published widely in the field of modern and contemporary British and Irish fiction, with special emphasis on the short story, women's writing and narrative theory. She is the author of a critical study on John Banville (Rodopi, 2004) and of *Irish Women Writers and the Modern Short Story* (Palgrave, 2016). She is also co-editor of several essay collections: *Unreliable Narration* (De Gruyter, 2008), *Irish Women Writers* (Lang, 2011), *Mary Lavin* (Irish Academic Press, 2013), *The Irish Short Story* (Lang, 2015) and *The Modern Short Story and Magazine Culture, 1880–1950* (Edinburgh University Press, 2021).

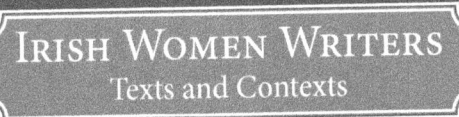

Ethel Colburn Mayne:
Selected Stories

Elke D'hoker

EER
Edward Everett Root, Publishers, Brighton, 2021.

EER
Edward Everett Root, Publishers, Co. Ltd.,
30 New Road, Brighton, Sussex, BN1 1BN, England.
www.eerpublishing.com

edwardeverettroot@yahoo.co.uk

Full details of our overseas agents in America, Australia, Canada, China, Europe, and Japan and how to order our books are given on our website.

Elke D'hoker: *Ethel Colburn Mayne: Selected Stories*

First published in Great Britain in 2021.

© Elke D'hoker 2021.

This edition © Edward Everett Root 2021.

ISBN: 9781913087296 Paperback
ISBN: 9781913087302 Hardback
ISBN: 9781913087241 eBook

Irish Women Writers. Texts and Contexts series, volume 2.

Elke D'hoker has asserted her right to be identified as the author of this Work in accordance with the Copyright, Designs and Patents Act 1988 as the owner of this Work.

All rights reserved. No part of this publication may be reproduced, stored in a retrieval system or transmitted in any form or by any means, electronic, mechanical, photocopying, recording or otherwise, without the prior permission of the copyright owner.

Production by Pageset Limited, High Wycombe, Buckinghamshire.

Contents

1. **Ethel Colburn Mayne: A Literary Life** 1
   Introduction 1
   An Irish New Woman 4
   Narrating Public Lives 9
   Documenting Inner Lives 12
   A London Literary Life 17

2. **Mayne's Short Fiction in Context** 21
   Fin-de-siècle Aestheticism 21
   New Woman Concerns 25
   Anglo-Irish Stories 28
   Modernism and Modernity 32
   A Note on the Selected Stories 36

3. **The Stories** 39
   The End of It 39
   Lucille 56
   Photographs 64
   The Boulevardiers 72
   Desertsurges 80
   The Turret-Room 100
   The Happy Day 121
   The Man of the House 133
   The Letter on the Floor 146
   The Peacocks 163

The Picnic 171

4. **Bibliography 181**
   Primary Sources 181
   Secondary Sources 187

Acknowledgements

I first came across Ethel Colburn Mayne's intriguing short stories in *The Yellow Book*. Eager to learn more about her, I spent many happy hours in the British Library reading her fascinating story collections and novels and became ever more indignant that this wonderful writer had been almost entirely forgotten. I am very grateful, therefore, to Kathryn Laing and Sinéad Mooney, editors of this *Irish Women Writers. Texts and Contexts* series, to encourage me to redress this neglect by publishing a selection of her stories. Working on a forgotten writer came with its own challenges, however, especially since I had little experience with archival research and the existing brief sketches of Mayne contained so many blanks and uncertainties. Susan Waterman came to my help at precisely the right moment and I cannot thank her enough for the generosity with which she shared the letters and other archival material concerning Mayne that she has assembled over the years. I really hope she writes that biography of Mayne very soon.

Permission to quote from archival material has been granted by the National Library of Scotland, the British Library, Macmillan and Co. Archives and the University of Reading, Special Collections.

Ethel Colburn Mayne: A Literary Life

Introduction

In 1957 the British writer and critic Christopher Isherwood edited *Great English Short Stories*, an anthology of "The Best" short stories published in Britain since the start of the twentieth century (Isherwood 1957, 10). The thirteen stories Isherwood selected have, by and large, become part of the short fiction canon and their authors will be familiar to most readers today: from Joseph Conrad and George Moore to Katherine Mansfield, D.H. Lawrence and V.S. Pritchett. One name in his selection, however, is probably unfamiliar to most readers, that of Ethel Colburn Mayne. Introducing Mayne's story, "The Man of the House", Isherwood praises it for its "delicacy and perception", its "honesty", and its "quite unladylike Irish wit" (Isherwood 1957, 250). In her own time, Mayne had several such champions among fellow writers and critics: Henry Harland coached her early writing for publication in *The Yellow Book,* Ford Madox Ford wrote in 1920, "now that Mr. James is dead, there seems to be only Miss Mayne in England who has the perception and the great skill to be the historian of this our fugitive day" (Hueffer 1920, 10), and Elizabeth Bowen included a story by Mayne in her 1936 anthology *The Faber Book of Modern Short Stories,* while noting in a later essay that Mayne "never quite [received] the prominence she deserved" (Bowen 1945, 139).

That verdict continues to hold true today. When Mayne's name is mentioned at all, it is as a contributor and sub-editor of *The Yellow Book* in 1895–96 even though she continued to write until the late 1930s.[1] In the course of these forty years, she published four novels, six collections of short fiction and six works of non-fiction, primarily biographies. She also worked as a critic and translated some eighteen books—poetry, fiction and non-fiction—from French and German as well as publishing numerous articles, essays and book reviews. During her lifetime she appears to have been best known as the author of celebrated biographies of Byron and Lady Byron, but today it is primarily her fiction that stands out as worthy of renewed attention.[2] Her novels offer fascinating depictions of talented and spirited young women struggling against the patriarchal restrictions and gendered conventions that hamper their quest for independence and self-definition. While this conflict between self and society also characterises other New Woman fiction of the period, the Anglo-Irish perspective Mayne brings to bear on this theme makes her novels unique testimonies of Protestant upper-middle-class life in small Irish naval and garrison towns around the turn of the twentieth century. At the same time, the explicitly female focus of her fiction makes it an interesting counterpart to the novels of George Moore as well as a forerunner to the novels of Elizabeth Bowen, Molly Keane and Jennifer Johnston.

In her short stories too, Mayne frequently foregrounds the experiences of genteel girls and women, yet as they span her entire career—from the 1890s to the 1930s—her stories range more widely in themes, settings and subject matter. At the same time, their brevity gives them the focus, unity and emotional tension

---

1. Her name—or the pseudonym she used for these early stories, Frances E. Huntley—thus crops up in studies of *The Yellow Book* (Hanson 1989, 17; Chan 2007, 64) as well as in Tina O'Toole's *The Irish New Woman*, where she is mentioned alongside writers such as Sarah Grand, George Egerton, L.T. Meade and Katherine Cecil Thurston (O'Toole 2016, 4).
2. Isherwood notes in his introduction, "Her books on Byron and Lady Byron are still regarded as standard works" (1957, 250).

that her novels sometimes lack. Taken in its entirety, moreover, Mayne's short fiction reflects not just her own development as a writer and the momentous changes that took place in women's lives around 1900, but also the changes the modern short story underwent from its popularity among New Women writers in *fin-de-siècle* Britain to the heyday of the modernist short story. In the context of the tradition of the Irish short story, therefore, Mayne's work presents a bridge between the short fiction of George Moore or George Egerton and the late modernist stories of Elizabeth Bowen, Norah Hoult and Seán O'Faoláin. Nevertheless, although Mayne always presented herself as Irish, her work has never been included in histories of Irish literature. As an Anglo-Irish Protestant writer who made a career for herself in London, she falls outside nationalist definitions of the Irish canon, especially since her relocation to England in the early twentieth century made her a bystander to precisely those political and cultural events that so strongly shaped that canon. Her work sits uneasily, therefore, with the dominant narrative of the Revival and its aftermath, nor does it fit the traditional conception of Irish modernism as international, experimental and male. The recent opening up of the canon of Irish modernism, however, will hopefully also create a space for Ethel Colburn Mayne as one of many fascinating authors whose work reflects the social upheavals of the early twentieth century in a variety of ways.[3]

The selection of short stories presented in this volume will help to play a part in this recovery, by introducing readers to Mayne's central themes as well as to the specific style she developed, in dialogue with the literary movements of the time. Before turning to the stories, however, I will introduce Mayne's life, her versatile literary output and its reception in the London press at the turn of the twentieth century.

---

3. For recent revisions of Irish modernism, see for instance Cleary 2014; Keown and Taaffe 2010. For a consideration of Mayne's place within this expanded version of Irish modernism, see D'hoker 2021.

An Irish New Woman

Ethelind Frances Colburn Mayne was born in Johnstown, a small village in County Kilkenny, on the 7th of January 1865. She was the second of eight children of Charles Edward Bolton Mayne and Charlotte Emily Henrietta Sweetman.[4] As a member of the Royal Irish Constabulary, her father was posted in different places, until he became a resident magistrate in Cork and the family settled in Blackrock. In a 1924 letter to the famous Edinburgh sculptor James Pittendrigh Macgillivray, Mayne describes her family history and defends her Irish credentials as follows:

> You are quite right about our being Norman. But the Irish blend of the Maynes went to Ireland under Elizabeth, so I think we may, very deferentially, call ourselves Irish! My mother <u>was</u> Irish—her name was Sweetman, and that name has been much concerned in what used to be called the "rebel" doings in Ireland. But my mother's father was in the British Army, one of the Lancer Regiments; and she herself was an ardent Unionist. She died in 1902. My father was first in the Royal Irish Constabulary, and afterwards a resident Magistrate—and so it was in the "British Garrison" circles that our social life in Ireland was spent.[5]

---

4. The family had eight children, only four of whom survived into adulthood: Charlotte Elizabeth (1863–1877); Ethelind Frances Colburn (1865–1941); Edward Colburn (1869–1959); Charles Sydney Bolton (1870); Edith Violet (1871–1941); Robert William Dawson (1873–?); John Theophilus Bolton (1874–1947); and Richard Hugh (1877). For this information as well as for all references to Mayne's letters in this introduction, I am exceedingly grateful to Susan Waterman, who is preparing a biography on Mayne, and has generously shared her material with me.

5. This letter, dated 1 August 1924, is part of Mayne's correspondence with James Pittendrigh Macgillivray in the mid-to-late 1920s. Mayne had first contacted him in March 1924 to ask for a photograph of his statue of Byron newly erected in Aberdeen to use in the 1924 edition of her Byron biography. The correspondence flourished for about a year and in January 1925, Macgillivray invited her to the Robert Burns dinner in London at which he was delivering

Mayne was educated in private schools in Ireland, becoming fluent in German and French. "If her novels are a reflection of her life as a young woman", Jad Adams notes, "she experienced with some irritation the confines of rural Irish life" (Adams 2006). Indeed, Mayne's fiction often stages sensitive and artistic girls and young women who feel themselves at odds with the coarse competition and asinine rituals of the "marriage market". Mayne herself was translating German poetry in the early 1890s and trying her hand at poetry and short fiction. She attentively followed the literary news from London and the continent and, in 1895, she sent a short story to *The Yellow Book,* the much-publicised new London journal, edited by Henry Harland and published by John Lane of The Bodley Head. Associated with Aestheticism and Decadence, the magazine was illustrated by Aubrey Beardsley and published short stories by Henry James, Hubert Crackanthorpe, Ernest Dowson and Arthur Symons as well as by New Woman writers like Ella D'Arcy, George Egerton, Netta Syrett and Evelyn Sharp.

In an unpublished memoir, "Reminiscences of Henry Harland", Mayne remembers her delight when her short story was accepted by *The Yellow Book,* with Harland "praising it in words which even now it thrills me to recall" (Samuels Lasner 2006, 18). The story was published, under the pen name of Frances E. Huntley, in the July 1895 issue, which also featured stories by James, Egerton, Arnold Bennett, Kenneth Grahame and Harland himself.[6] Mayne's delight was even greater when,

---

the address. In one of the last letters of the collection, dated 12 January 1927, Mayne tells him of the devastating death of her father, and the last letter is two months later, in which she gives him her new address, at her sister's in Richmond, Surrey. The letters are part of the "Correspondence and papers of James Pittendrigh Macgillivray" (Acc. 3501), quoted by permission of the National Library of Scotland.

6. Mayne would write about this pseudonym that it was "almost the only circumstance in my life of which I am thoroughly ashamed" (Samuels Lasner 2006, 24).

after several months of further correspondence, Harland offered her the position of sub-editor to *The Yellow Book*, to replace Ella D'Arcy who had left for Paris. Though Harland called the post "derisory", Mayne comments "I need not enlarge on how little derisory it seemed to a girl who had lived all her life until this in Ireland, and was entirely unknown to the literary world" (Samuels Lasner 2006, 18). Judging from her "Reminiscences", the months she spent working together with Harland on *The Yellow Book* were an exciting and formative experience for Mayne: she became familiar with the London literary scene, met prominent writers, learnt the craft of editing and was instructed by Harland in the aesthetics of the modern short story. When D'Arcy returned from Paris in April 1896, Mayne was rather unceremoniously ousted from her position and she returned to Cork.[7] Yet the experience gave her the courage she needed to embark on a writing career.

---

7. Anne M. Windholz (1996, 123) refers to the episode, quoting from a letter by D'Arcy in which she boasts about removing Mayne's story from the forthcoming issue: "I'm completely revising [Harland's] Contents-list, just according to my fancy! I found 'The Only Way' with that idiot Frances E. Huntley [Ethel Colburne [*sic*] Mayne] was to leave her out altogether; and I've also, kindly, expunged her name from the Yellow Dwarf's mistaken eulogies. He will, certainly, murder me when he discovers it." The "Yellow Dwarf" was the pseudonym under which Harland wrote his editorial columns. Windholz (1996, 130) suggests that the "virulence" of D'Arcy's attack on Mayne was at least partly due to "indignation that Mayne, however temporarily, had been chosen to replace her as sub-editor". Mayne herself notes in her "Reminiscences", "There was to have been a third [story]; it had been accepted, printed, and the proofs corrected by me; but it never was allowed to go in" (Samuels Lasner 2006, 24). For an account of the incident from Mayne's perspective, see also Waterman 1999, 191.

The experience of being suddenly dismissed from a work position found its way into two of Mayne's short stories, "The Separate Room" and "The Letter on the Floor". In both stories, there is also a romantic entanglement (implicit in the first, explicit in the second) between the young woman and her older, married employer. Mayne's admiration for Harland clearly comes through in her "Reminiscences" as well as in her defense of him in a discussion with A.R. Orage in *The New Age* (R.H.C. 1918b; c).

The stories Mayne published in *The Yellow Book* and *Chapman's Magazine of Fiction* between 1895 and 1897 formed the basis for her first collection of short stories, *The Clearer Vision*, which was published by the London publisher T. Fisher Unwin in 1898.[8] The title alludes to Harland's conviction that the short story should express "a perception that penetrated beyond the surface of things and people, a shaft sunk in our common consciousness, a theme that reached farther than the experience it transcribed [...] the 'clearer vision' of a consciousness humbly alive to its waiting presence" (Samuels Lasner 2006, 22). Mayne's stories in *The Clearer Vision* bear the stamp of Harland's poetics. The stories highlight the conflicting shades of emotions and thoughts of young men and women that can never be adequately expressed in the stilted conversation of courtship or social intercourse. Following Harland's dictum "*Cultivez l'art d'omettre*", the stories convey this rich inner life through the use of ellipsis, implication and interior monologue. In some stories this is taken too far, causing a reviewer for *The Saturday Review* to complain that "the meaning [is] so coy that when it is dragged out it irritates by proving worth less than the trouble of delving" (Anon. 1898a, 544). This is seconded by a review in *The Athenaeum* which grants Mayne "real talent", but counsels her to "give up the extensive use of French scraps and disjointed fragments of phrase" (Anon. 1898b, 606). In the collection's best stories, however, the sustained introspection casts a moving and intriguing light on the inner lives of young women and their struggles with the Victorian expectations of marriage, motherhood and conventional femininity. *The Bookman* rightly

---

8. "A Pen-and-Ink Effect", first published in the July 1895 issue of *The Yellow Book*, was reprinted (and slightly rewritten) as part of the story "The End of It" in *The Clearer Vision*. "Lucille", part of "Two Stories", published in the January 1896 issue, was reprinted as a separate story in the collection. Mayne published three stories in *Chapman's Magazine of Fiction*: "Her Story and His" (November 1895), "His Glittering Hour" (April 1896) and "Unto the Shore of Nothing" (May 1897). Mayne rewrote this last story for incorporation into the three-part story "On the Programme: Three Ball-Room Studies" of *The Clearer Vision*.

singles out the opening story, "Herb of Grace", as having "a power and completeness positively fearsome" as well as "piercing accuracy of delineation". The reviewer continues, "[t]here are phrases—sentences—on these pages positively startling in their unshrinking fidelity. Undoubtedly 'Herb of Grace' is a striking and an able and a clearsighted bit of work, more than sufficient to justify the somewhat ambitious title of the volume" (Anon. 1898c, 87).

Back in Cork, Mayne was also working in other literary genres. In 1902 she won a prize given by *The Academy and Literature* for the poem "May Day at Sea", and her first novel, *Jessie Vandeleur*, was published by George Allen. Featuring an Irish girl who moves to London after coming into an inheritance, the novel paints an ironic, almost satiric, picture of the artistic circles Mayne must have mingled in during her work for *The Yellow Book*. An ambitious and rebellious "New Woman", Jessie wants to succeed in these circles not just for her beauty, but also for her brains. She brilliantly finishes the novel her Irish fiancé had been writing and publishes it as her own work, gaining the love of the celebrated aestheticist writer Deyncourt. She even keeps his love after the death of her fiancé exposes her literary theft. Yet, the reader, who is also given the perspective of the fiancé and his family, is likely to be more critical of the heroine. The novel tackles many aestheticist and New Woman themes—the relation between art and life, gender and art, men and women— but the shifting focalisation makes it often difficult to pinpoint the author's stance on these themes. Mayne's excessively allusive style tends to obscure the novel's meaning in places. As a reviewer for *The Academy and Literature* put it: "Here and there in the book the carefully built sentences are successful, and result in the clear utterance of certain subtle and evasive thoughts and feelings. But, on the whole, the story has been killed by affectation of style, and by successful effort to avoid all simplicity of manner" (Anon. 1903, 32).

Narrating Public Lives

After the retirement of her father in 1905, Mayne moved with him and her married sister to London. There her literary career branched out in different directions. Two years earlier she had met C.F. Cazenove of The Literary Agency of London, who would become her agent for the next ten years. He placed some of her stories in *The Pall Mall Magazine* and secured a contract for her next novel, *The Fourth Ship*, with Chapman and Hall.[9] This London publisher would also publish Mayne's two other novels and three of her story collections. *The Fourth Ship* returns to some of the themes of her first novel, but omits the contrived elusiveness and problematic heroine that had been criticised in *Jessie Vandeleur*. Instead, *The Fourth Ship* offers an astute, complex portrayal of the lives of late-nineteenth-century Anglo-Irish women, by juxtaposing two heroines: the shy, self-effacing Josephine St. Lawrence who becomes a governess in impoverished circumstances and her friend—and former love rival—Millicent North, a spirited woman and brilliant pianist who nevertheless sacrifices her artistic ambitions for a conventional life as wife and mother.[10] The final part of the novel moves from this rather depressing portrait of late-nineteenth-century womanhood to the next generation through Millie's three daughters. Although the eldest two seem set on paths that replicate both Josephine's dreary spinsterhood and Millie's frustrated domesticity, the youngest daughter Chris, short for Christabel, embodies the hope that the late-nineteenth-century changes to women's lives might hold a more fulfilling life in store for her. *The Fourth Ship* was well

---

9. Mayne published four stories in *The Pall Mall Magazine*: "The Invitation to the Valse" (1907), "Your New Hat" (1909), "As a Lamb…" (1911) and "The Colonel" (1912).
10. Talented musicians recur frequently in Mayne's novels and stories. In a letter of 4 September 1924 to Macgillivray, Mayne reveals the biographical background behind this interest: "I used to play the piano very well, and I used to sing with a melting mezzo-soprano—so there! My mother was an exquisite pianist—could have made a career, if she hadn't married."

received in the press, with the reviewer of *The Athenaeum* calling it "the finest and most finished work of fiction [he had] read for many years" (Anon. 1908, 932) and *The Daily Telegraph* recommending it as a "sheer delight" for the reader "to whom character, observation, literary sincerity, and true feeling are of more value than many adventures" (quoted in Waterman 1999, 194).

The following years brought further successes for Mayne. Methuen published her biographical study, *Enchanters of Men*, in 1909. It contains portraits of "fair, frail, fascinating—and foreign, ladies", as Mayne puts it in the preface (Mayne 1909, v). They are mostly royals, mistresses and artists who have been overlooked in history in favour of the more famous men in their lives. On the basis of the success of this book—Mayne was praised as "the ideal pen portrait-painter" in *The Academy* (W.W.T. 1909, 395)—the publishing firm of Hutchinson commissioned Mayne to write a study of the royal house of Monaco, *The Romance of Monaco and Its Rulers* (1910), and Methuen contracted her to write a biography of Byron. Mayne spent four years researching and writing Byron's life and her insightful biography was published in two volumes in both London and New York in 1912. It received widespread acclaim and became the work by which Mayne would continue to be identified. *The English Review* called the biography "ample, careful, and highly intelligent" (Anon 1913a, 323) and *The Bookman* argued that it had "superseded all others", while singling out for special praise "its discussion of the love episodes", for "the feminine point of view" which she brought to them and their combination of "a woman's innate sympathy and delicacy of feeling with a breadth of mind and a knowledge of the world which are less generally characteristic of the sex" (Douglas 1912, 188–89).

If Mayne was praised for her even-handed and objective treatment of Byron, her subsequent work of non-fiction, *Browning's Heroines* (1913), was criticised for being too feminist. Chatto and Windus had commissioned her to write a study of the women in Browning's poetry, a topic which greatly interested her.

As Mayne notes in the preface, she had become an ardent admirer of Browning's poetry under the influence of Henry Harland who was always "reading, quoting, declaiming, almost breathing, Browning" (Mayne 1913, viii). Through a detailed analysis of several of his poems, Mayne celebrates Browning as "the first 'feminist' poet since Shakespeare" because of his depiction of brave and strong women. Again, the work met with positive reviews, even though reviewers were uneasy about the feminist label she applied to Browning. A reviewer for *The Saturday Review*, for instance, calls *Browning's Heroines* "the most excellent book of commentary upon Browning we have seen since Mr. G.K. Chesterton wrote upon this poet the best book of his life. The author answers the call of genius with a clear call of her own" (Anon. 1913b, 685). Yet he adds, "[t]he author of this book is a feminist, and she does not hesitate to claim that Browning, also, was a feminist. If we have a fault to find with this book, it is just this introduction of a foolish label, equally unjust to the author herself and to her subject." A reviewer for *The Athenaeum*, on the other hand, praises Mayne's original readings, noting that her "enthusiasm for her subject has not impaired her critical faculty" (Anon. 1913c, 616).

Given the upheavals of the suffragette movement in the early twentieth century, feminism may well have been on Mayne's mind during these years. In "Your New Hat", one of her stories published in *The Pall Mall Magazine* (1909), a young girl tries to square her delight in fashion, dances and men with her support for the suffragettes; the two novels Mayne was writing around this time also have a more outspokenly feminist quality than her earlier work. *Gold Lace: A Study of Girlhood* (1913) tells of Rhoda Henry, a spirited English girl, who is sent to visit relatives in an Irish garrison town after breaking off with her fiancé. In Ireland she is shocked by the insensitive way the military men—the "gold lace" of the title—treat the local girls: courting and then discarding them without a further thought. Rhoda refuses to play that game and persuades the local Anglo-Irish girls to follow suit.

In a review for *The Bookman,* Frank Swinnerton called Mayne "a really delicate observer, who does not shirk from the conclusions to which she is brought", praising "her illuminating discussion of the significance of women in the world" (Swinnerton 1913, 174–5).[11] Mayne's fourth novel, *One of Our Grandmothers* (1916), applies that feminist scrutiny to the life of an earlier generation of women. In this novel, Mayne returns to the world of *The Fourth Ship* to explore further how the supremely talented pianist Millicent North was thwarted in her ambition to carve out an independent life as a piano teacher and was forced to settle for marriage and motherhood instead. While *The Fourth Ship* is a rather sprawling novel, covering several generations of women, *One of Our Grandmothers* is an admirably focused and moving portrait of a tragic heroine for whom the achievements of the women's movement sadly came too late.

Documenting Inner Lives

Although the novel received positive reviews, it was the last one Mayne would publish. Instead, she chose to devote herself to the short story form. In 1910, she had published a second collection, *Things That No One Tells,* and in the years that followed, she placed a number of stories in *The Pall Mall Magazine, The Nation* and *Vanity Fair.*[12] After Mayne gave up writing longer fiction, however, her short story collections followed one another in quick

11. In a survey of book reviewing in the interwar periodical press, Claire Battershill describes Swinnerton as a "prolific novelist", whose "influence on the literary culture of the 1920s and 1930s was profound". He disliked romance and "tended to recommend works of non-fiction and serious literary novels to his readers" (2018, 18).
12. The stories published in *The Nation* and *Vanity Fair* in the early 1910s would be published in the collection *Come In*: "Dispossession" and "Vanity" are sections of the story "Three Rooms"; "Four Dances" and "Atherley" are sections of the story "Four Ballrooms". *The Nation* (1907–1923) was a quite radical, liberal magazine, edited by H.W. Massingham. It would merge with *The Athenaeum* in 1923, becoming *The Nation and Athenaeum* (Havighurst 1974, 143–225).

succession: *Come In* (1917), *Blindman* (1919), *Nine of Hearts* (1923) and *Inner Circle* (1925). In the same period, Mayne also contributed stories and essays to modernist little magazines. In 1918, Ezra Pound asked her to write an essay about Henry James for a special issue of *The Little Review* dedicated to James, who had passed away two years earlier. One of the most famous American modernist magazines, *The Little Review* published work by T.S. Eliot, Sherwood Anderson, Gertrude Stein and William Carlos Williams and, notoriously, serialised *Ulysses* between 1918 and 1921 (Golding 2012). In her essay, Mayne reminisced about James's association with Henry Harland and the other *Yellow Book* writers in the 1890s, while explaining James's aesthetics and assessing his career (Mayne 1918, 1–4). The essay drew a scornful response from A.R. Orage, the editor of the London-based socialist magazine *The New Age*. Orage argued that James never really aligned himself with "the writers of the famous 'Yellow Book', of whom Miss Mayne was not the least characteristic" (R.W.C. 2018a, 365). Rather, he claims, their paths only briefly crossed before diverging again: while James's fame rose to further heights, *The Yellow Book* proved to be a "literary cul-de-sac" (R.W.C. 2018a, 366). Mayne took issue with this verdict in a letter to the editor, which lead to a lively discussion in two subsequent issues of *The New Age* about the relative merits of the literary generation preceding that of Orage himself (R.W.C. 2018b; 2018c). The conversation sheds interesting light on the perception of Harland, James and Nineties Decadence in the early decades of the twentieth century, but also reflects Mayne's own standing as a writer and critic of note within the British and international modernist literary set of the time.[13] Further evidence of this can be found, for instance, in her contribution to a collection of essays about the French modernist, Marcel Proust, where she appears in

---

13. Given the explicitly socialist concerns of *The New Age* (G.B. Shaw was heavily involved in the magazine), it is not surprising that the aestheticist and decadent movement should get short shrift in its pages (see Scholes).

the company of authors like Arnold Bennett, Joseph Conrad and Clive Bell (Mayne 1923, 90–95).

In the early 1920s Mayne's own stories started to appear in several modernist publications as well. Between 1922 and 1924, she published "Stripes", "The Shirt of Nessus" and "Humour" in the short-lived *The Golden Hind: A Quarterly of Art and Literature*, in the company of Naomi Mitchison, Aldous Huxley, Dorothy Richardson and Graham Greene (Rogers 2009, 579–58). "Black Magic" appeared in *The Westminster Gazette*, which also published short stories by Mansfield, D.H. Lawrence and Saki. In 1924 Ford Madox Ford asked her for stories for his magazine *The Transatlantic Review*, which featured work by such well-known modernist writers as Ezra Pound, H.D., Gertrude Stein, James Joyce and Ernest Hemingway (Gasiorek 2012, 697ff.). Mayne's two contributions, "Dialogue in a Cab" and "The Difference" were published in the February and May issues, respectively. In 1926, Mayne contributed a story, "The Lower Road", to *Atalanta's Garland: Being the Book of the Edinburgh University Women's Union*, which also contained work by Katherine Mansfield and Virginia Woolf.[14]

If Mayne was never a central player in British modernist circles, her inclusion in these magazines and anthologies nevertheless reflects the respect and regard for her work within these circles. This is affirmed by Katherine Mansfield's positive review of *Blindman* in the pages of *The Athenaeum*. Concurring with Mayne's preference for character and psychology over intricate plot development, Mansfield notes how Mayne is interested "not in the event itself", but "in what happens immediately after", in the effect of the event on the character's mind (K.M. 1920, 48). The title of Mayne's second collection, *Things That No One Tells*,

---

14. *Atalanta's Garland* was "a special issue magazine to celebrate the twenty-first anniversary of the opening of Edinburgh University Women's Union, and to raise funds for the development of the Union"; it offered a "miscellany of short stories, poems, articles, and reproductions of artworks", reflecting "the achievement of women in various areas of public life" (Binckes and Snyder 2019, 437).

also alludes to this introspective bent that characterises most of her short fiction. As in her debut collection, the stories mostly tell of the friendships and courtships of genteel young women, both in England and in Ireland. In these stories, however, Mayne has moved away from the often excessively allusive and elliptical style of her first collection towards a more precisely observed form of realism that nevertheless retains its focus on the characters' thoughts and feelings, which can never adequately be expressed or communicated. In her subsequent collections, Mayne would widen her thematic scope but retain her poetic focus on the finer shades of mood or the intricate conflicts of feeling.

For Ford Madox Ford, Mayne's stories accurately record everyday lives, telling "of minute hourly embarrassments; of sympathetic or unsympathetic personal contacts; of little-marked successes and failures, of queer jealousies, of muted terminations" (Hueffer 1920, 10–11). He compares Mayne's work favourably with that of Henry James, a verdict that is echoed by Frank Swinnerton, who argues that the difference between the two lies in Mayne's exceptional visualising power:

> [*Come In*] is not romantic, as Henry James's books are: it is scientific and selective. Miss Mayne saves herself from the charge of indiscretion in 'telling' what one feels she has discovered by her own sympathy and divination; she dexterously and wonderfully makes us see the things that happened and come to our own conclusions. That is her quite special talent, that there is not a sentence but has its implication and reverberation. (Swinnerton 1918, 158)

Mayne's talent for illuminating character, while also present in her last two novels, seemed to find an even better application in her short fiction, where small suggestive details serve to conjure up characters with remarkable complexity and depth. As *The English Review* notes in a review of *Inner Circle*

Mayne has, more, perhaps, than any living writer, the animistic secret; she gives with delicate authenticity that running commentary of unspoken thought which is universal and so continuous in all human life [...]. In her hands the quick soul has even more importance than the persona; the drama is seen behind the retina of the spectator, and becomes, therefore, immeasurably complex, a complexity, however, that this remarkable writer has the power of presenting as a broadly lit whole. (Anon. 1925, 685)

If comparisons with James dominated the early reviews, subsequent reviewers would often make connections with Katherine Mansfield. *The Spectator* remarks that it has become "the obvious thing for reviewers to talk of Miss Mayne in connexion with Katherine Mansfield" (Anon. 1923a, 22). The reviewer grants both writers "a deep insight into the minds of women and children", yet attributes to Mayne a more deliberate sense of "scheme" and structure: she works "threads into the warp and weft with cunning hands; and the result is stories of exquisite and perfect design". The review concludes, "[w]e cannot help feeling that her style has been brought to its state of perfection by the limpid and disciplined spirit of pity which is the moving power behind her work." The comparison with Mansfield seems to have become so widespread that in an advertisement for *Nine of Hearts*, the publishers call Mayne "the only short-story writer capable of succeeding Katherine Mansfield" (Anon 1923b, 4).

Another way to gauge the esteem in which Mayne's short fiction was held is to look at the stories that were reprinted in anthologies up until the 1950s.[15] As mentioned already, "The Man of the House" was selected by Elizabeth Bowen for her *Faber Book of Modern Short Stories* and by Christopher Isherwood for his *Great English Short Stories*. Edward J. O'Brien picked her stories twice

---

15. For a list of these anthologised stories, see the Bibliography. It is possible that other stories by Mayne have appeared in anthologies that have escaped my notice.

for his renowned *Best British Short Stories* anthology: "Stripes" was published in the 1923 volume and "Ugliness" was included in the 1931 collection. Similarly, Arthur Waugh of Chapman and Hall chose Mayne three times for inclusion in the firm's *Georgian Stories* series of anthologies published in the 1920s. "Lovells Meeting" was included in the 1922 volume, "The Picnic" appeared in the 1926 volume and "The Lower Road" in that of 1927, next to a story by Liam O'Flaherty. Equally mindful perhaps of Mayne's Irish background, the anthology *31 Stories by Thirty and One Authors*, included Mayne's "The Turret-Room" alongside "The Whiteboys" by Somerville and Ross. Dorothy L. Sayers, for her part, chose "The Separate Room", a story from *Come In*, for her 1928 anthology, *Great Short Stories of Detection, Mystery and Crime* and "The Shirt of Nessus" was included in *The Uncertain Element: An Anthology of Fantastic Conceptions* (1950).

A London Literary Life

The favourable reception of her short stories added to Mayne's already celebrated status as biographer to make her a well-established literary figure in the 1920s and early 1930s. Two of her closest friends were the writers Mary Butts and Violet Hunt. Mayne had met Hunt during her brief stint as sub-editor at *The Yellow Book* and the two women would remain intimate friends for the rest of their lives. In 1921 they were both actively involved with the founding of PEN, the international writers' organisation. Mayne was to have been Hunt's literary executor but Hunt, though suffering from dementia for many years, outlived her friend. Butts and Mayne probably met during the First World War and they also became fast friends, with Butts recognising that she had found "a soulmate" in Mayne (Blondel 1998, 65). One of Butts's diary entries, following a dinner party in 1931 with Mayne (and Butts's husband, Gabriel Atkin), gives a sense of Mayne's generosity and kindness:

linked laughter between the three of us—like Mozart. All that it has been to be with her again. [...] What I became aware of listening to Ethel, not only the argument *and* the voice, but all of her, the impact of her love and wit and imagination. An experience I shall never lose, and learn to use again with other people. [...] The Harmony between G and I was her work, and the next day's joy and the life's memory. (quoted in Blondel 1998, 271)

Butts dedicated her first short story collection to Mayne, in recognition of her friend's advice and encouragement. Mayne also made a case for Butts's novel, *Death of Felicity Taverner,* to be added to the British shortlist for the Fémina Vie Heureuse prize in 1933 (Blondel 1998, 310). Mayne had been involved with the English judging panel for the Fémina prize since its formation around 1919, serving as president in 1924 and 1925. In those years, the prize was awarded to Percy Lubbock's *Roman Pictures* and E.M. Forster's *A Passage to India,* respectively.

Mayne's own fiction output, however, dwindled after the publication of *Inner Circle* in 1925. A few stories continued to appear in periodicals, including "Ugliness" in *The New Statesman* in 1930[16] and "A Bit of Her" in *Life and Letters* in 1935.[17] Susan Waterman suggests that caring for her elderly father may have been too much of a drain on her energy (Waterman 1999, 199). Moreover, Mayne took on more work as a translator in these years in order to provide for their household. This became even more pressing after her father's death in 1927 and the loss of his pension. Among the many books which Mayne translated from French and German, her translation of several of Freud's articles

---

16. For a discussion of this story in the context of *The New Statesman*, see Abu-Manneh 2011, 130–1.
17. *Life and Letters* was a literary review founded by Desmond MacCarthy after he had left *The New Statesman* in 1928. It published prominent Bloomsbury modernists (e.g. Woolf, Forster, Sackville-West) as well as writers like Cyril Connolly, Seán O'Faoláin and Edith Wharton (Goldman, 2009).

for the five-volume Hogarth Press edition of the *Collected Papers of Sigmund Freud* (1924–25) stands out.[18] Mayne probably owed this commission to her acquaintance with Joan Riviere, a leading British psychoanalyst and prominent member of the British Psychoanalytic Society. In her letter of 30 June 1924 to Macgillivray, Mayne mentions, "I do a good deal of translation for her [Joan Riviere] for the Society's Journal [the *International Journal of Psycho-Analysis*]", adding, "[s]he is the 'Mrs. Luttrell' of my story 'Light'". To another correspondent Mayne reports that Riviere showed one of her stories to Ernest Jones, who apparently "expressed an admiration quite extraordinary for the treatment, and [...] the insight [she] had brought to bear upon the theme".[19] The impact of Mayne's in-depth exploration of psychoanalysis on her short story collections of the 1920s certainly awaits further exploration.

In the late 1920s, Mayne worked on a biography of Lady Byron, for which she was given full access to previously unpublished family papers. When *The Life and Letters of Anne Isabella, Lady Noel Byron* was published in 1929, it attracted considerable attention for the epistolary evidence it procured of Byron's rumoured incestuous relation with his half-sister Augusta as well as his cruel treatment of his wife. The book was widely praised for its insightful and engaging portrait of Lady Byron and considered a worthy companion piece to Mayne's earlier Byron biography. Leonard Woolf commends it in *The Nation* as "one of the most fascinating and important biographies which have appeared for a long time",

---

18. Mayne translated five of the essays in the second volume of *Sigmund Freud: Collected Papers*, authorised translation under the supervision of Joan Riviere, to wit: "'Civilized' Sexual Morality and Modern Nervousness" (with E.B. Herford); "Psychogenic Visual Disturbance according to Psycho-Analytical Conceptions"; "Types of Neurotic Nosogenesis"; "The Predisposition to Obsessional Neurosis" (with Edward Glover) and "Infantile Mental Life" as well as two essays in the fourth volume: "Thoughts for the Times on War and Death" and "Some Character-Types met with in Psycho-Analytic Work" (Riviere 1924, 76–99; 105–112; 113–121; 122–132; 144–149; and Riviere 1925, 288–344).

19. Letter to Katharine Dexter McCormick, 13 January 1921, private collection of Susan Waterman. The story alluded to is probably "Light".

and Rebecca West hails it in *The Bookman* as the "most popular book of the London season" (quoted in Waterman 1999, 196–7). The last book which Mayne published was a biographical study of the love affair between Lord Granville and Lady Bessborough, the mother of the Anglo-Irish author Lady Caroline Lamb. *A Regency Chapter: Lady Bessborough and Her Friendships* (1939) was well-received, encouraging her to ask Macmillan's Lovat Dickson if the firm might be interested in either a novel she had recently completed or a collection of stories, the latter comprising "two 'long-shorts', and three shorter ones, two of which have been published serially".[20] Although she submitted manuscripts of both to Macmillan in early 1940, the novel was declined and the story collection was never published (Waterman 1999, 200).[21]

During the London Blitz, on 30 September 1940, the Twickenham house in which Mayne lived with her sister was bombed. Both women were hospitalised, Mayne for six weeks, and when they had sufficiently recovered, they left London for Torquay to be closer to their brothers. Yet their stay in Torquay was a short one, for Mayne died on 30 April 1941, within a few weeks of her sister. The death certificate notes "syncope" and "coronary thrombosis" as the causes of death, but Isherwood (1957, 250) mentions that she died of the after-effects of injuries received during the Blitz.[22]

---

20. Letter to Lovat Dickson, 13 March 1940. Quoted by permission of the University of Reading, Special Collections.
21. Among the Macmillan Archives at the British Library is a ledger containing a reader's report on "Sentence of Life" by Ethel Colburn Mayne, written by Phyllis Hartnoll, a poet and book editor, dated 3 February 1940. From the plot summary given in the report, the novel seems very different from Mayne's other novels: it revolves around the death of a girl who had been involved with a married barrister (later a judge), who is officially acquitted of her murder, but continues to be haunted by guilt and eventually commits suicide. Hartnoll considered it an unlikely and "unsatisfactory" story. Quoted by permission of the British Library, Macmillan and Co. Archives.
22. Death certificate, registered on 2 May 1941 in the District of Newton Abbot, Sub-district of Torquay, Devon.

Mayne's Short Fiction in Context

Fin-de-Siècle Aestheticism

In 1895, when Mayne submitted her first story to *The Yellow Book*, the genre of the short story was on the rise in the London literary scene. In 1888, Rudyard Kipling published *Plain Tales from the Hills*, often hailed as the first modern British short story collection; a few years later, the new magazine *The Strand* made the publication of self-contained individual stories its main selling-point (Chan 2007, 2–3). Many periodicals followed suit, which made the short story in the 1890s not just a fashionable genre but also a lucrative form for a writer to engage with (Baldwin, 2013, 9–11). As H.G. Wells later recalled, "[t]he 'nineties was a good and stimulating period for a short-story writer […] Short stories broke out everywhere" (Wells 1992, 165). Moreover, as Henry James noted in 1898, the short story was widely discussed by authors and critics, becoming "an object of such almost extravagant dissertation" (James 1898, 652). Contemporary critics were eager to point out the novelty and modernity of the genre, emphasising its distinction both from the novel and from the Victorian tale. While the tale had often been quite long, elaborately plotted and drawn to the fantastical, the exotic or the didactic, the modern short story was characterised by unity, concision and realism. No longer a condensed novel or "a mere story which is short", the short story came to be recognized as a separate genre, with an "essential unity of impression" as its chief characteristic (Matthews, 1994, 73). Brevity, in other words, came to be seen as a positive quality, with writers realising that "a short story could achieve great richness and complexity as a result of, rather than in spite of, its brevity" (Hunter, 2007, 2).

Although most of the popular stories that appeared in periodicals applied these demands of brevity, unity and "unique or single *effect*" (Poe, 1994, 61) to established plot patterns of romance, detection and adventure, more "literary" writers sought to elevate the short story to the highest art form. Henry James separated the two traditions through the "distinct effects [...] produced by this rigour of brevity":

> The one with which we are most familiar is that of the detached incident, single and sharp, as clear as a pistol-shot; the other, of rarer performance, is that of the impression, comparatively generalized—simplified, foreshortened, reduced to a single perspective—of a complexity or a continuity. The former is an adventure comparatively safe, in which you have, for the most part, but to put one foot in front of the other. It is just the risks of the latter, on the contrary, that make the best of the sport. (James 1898, 652)

With James's stories as his prime example, Henry Harland set out to make the second type of short story the spearhead of the elite, aestheticist poetics of *The Yellow Book*. In an essay for *The Athenaeum*, "Concerning the Short Story", he argues that "impression", rather than plot, should be the kernel of every short story: "[y]ou start with an impression and you endeavour to express your impression with the greatest possible economy of means" (Harland 1897, 6). In one of his "Yellow Dwarf" editorials for *The Yellow Book*, he characterises these literary stories as "delicate, distinguished, aristocratic", going on to claim, "their touch is light, their movement is deft and fleet", "they proceed by omission, by implication and suggestion" and use "the *demi-mot* and the *nuance*" (Harland 1896, 16).

Mayne's early stories clearly show the influence of Harland's short story poetics. "Lucille", which first appeared as part of "Two Stories" in the January 1896 issue of *The Yellow Book* and was later included in *The Clearer Vision*, consists in its entirety of the male narrator's imperfectly understood impressions of a female poet, Lucille Silverdale. "On the Programme: Three Ball-Room Studies", another story from *The Clearer Vision,* juxtaposes three impressionistic scenes from different dances a young woman is attending. The three scenes offer finely observed pictures of strictly codified male-female flirtations in the ball-room, but the connections between the scenes are omitted, which leaves the reader to supply the plot development Mayne only hints at. Stories told in separate scenes were fashionable at the *fin de siècle* and Mayne also uses the technique in "Herb of Grace" and "Ritournelle" from *The Clearer Vision* as well as in "The Red Umbrella" and "Madeline Annesley" from *Things That No One Tells*.[1] All of these stories depict the maturation process of a young woman—and the courtships she is involved in—through a series of detailed scenes, but what happens in between these scenes is only vaguely implied, so that plot is de-emphasized in favour of psychology and mood.

Following Harland's precepts, Mayne relies heavily on ellipsis, association and implication in these first two collections, so as to suggest rather than state meaning. These literary techniques receive an added thematic dimension, however, because of the way they seem to mirror the half-hints, meaningful glances and half-finished sentences that characterise the courtship rituals depicted

---

1. George Egerton uses the same technique of juxtaposing discrete scenes to suggest psychological development in such "tri-partite stories" as "Under Northern Sky", "The Regeneration of Two" and "A Psychological Moment at Three Periods" (D'hoker 2016, 27).

in the stories, which often leave the young protagonists in the dark about the true meaning of compliments or the real intention behind flirtations. The strongly coded artificiality of male-female intercourse in late-Victorian genteel society is evident, for instance, in "The End of It". Although its female protagonist delights, to some extent, in this performance of femininity ("It was such fun, all this pretending—these airs and graces, these sudden, premeditated fits of absence of mind, these deprecations, these humilities"), she also struggles to locate her own feelings, and those of her suitor, behind this "gay pretence" (p.42 in this volume). That misunderstanding is highly likely is also suggested by the discrepancy between the girl's reading of the "affair"—and the letter which summarises it—and that of the man in the second part of the story, "A Pen-and-Ink Effect". Such shifts of perspective are a recurring technique in Mayne's early stories: they also feature in the three stories Mayne published in *Chapman's Magazine*, with the title of "Her Story and His" clearly suggesting the distinction between both perspectives and the misunderstanding to which the lack of true communication gives rise.

More generally, this impressionistic filtering of events through a character's consciousness is a central component of *The Yellow Book*'s proto-modernist poetics, part of its attempt to distinguish the psychological "literary" story from its more popular, plotted counterpart. The resulting emphasis on the inner life of a character would remain a hallmark of Mayne's short fiction to the end and helps to explain the comparisons with the short fiction of Henry James and, later, Katherine Mansfield in reviews of her work. In most stories, this effect of interiority is realised through the use of sustained focalisation, through one, two, or, more rarely, several characters. The narratorial "telling" of the Victorian tale thus gives way to "showing" through free indirect discourse and quoted speech. In other stories, however, the subjective vision is realised through the use of unreliable first-person narrators, who unwittingly betray their presumptions and misunderstandings to the reader. In *The Clearer Vision*, this narrative technique is used in three stories—"One Near One", "The Lost Leader" and "Lucille"—which self-reflexively raise the question of whether it is at all possible (or desirable) to really understand another person.[2] In both "The Lost Leader" and "Lucille", the mysterious other is a supremely original, clever, and talented young woman (in "Lucille" she's even a published poet), who seems to throw away her talents—or so the narrators feel—by marrying a very mediocre man.[3] Although this judgement is questioned in "Lucille" by the exaggerated aestheticist pretension of the male narrator, the real motivation behind Lucille's decision remains a mystery to the reader.[4]

New Woman Concerns

The conflict hinted at in "Lucille", between marriage and motherhood, on the one hand, and artistic ambition, on the other, is also explored in the opening story of *The Clearer Vision*, "Herb of Grace". Adela, the protagonist of this story, is shown to lack any maternal instinct and to rebel against the social role that is expected of her. Instead, she devotes her energy to her "story-children", becoming a published author (Mayne 1898, 35). Nevertheless, after some agonising soul-searching, she does end up accepting a proposal of marriage from a man who considers "lady novelist[s] a mistake" and she rather dramatically burns her stories (Mayne 1898, 38). While the story's ending is ambiguous,

---

2. See my essay "A Forgotten Irish Modernist: Ethel Colburn Mayne", forthcoming in *Irish Modernisms: Gaps, Conjectures, Possibilities*, edited by Paul Fagan, John Greaney, and Tamara Radak, for a more detailed reading of this theme in the stories from *The Clearer Vision*.
3. Several years later, Mayne would rewrite "The Lost Leader" as "Gold Hair", a story included in the 1923 collection *Nine of Hearts*.
4. In its use of an unreliable male writer-narrator with aestheticist pretensions, "Lucille" also resembles George Egerton's story "A Lost Masterpiece", which was published in the first issue of *The Yellow Book* (Ledger 2007, 18).

it is clear that artistic ambitions and marriage, or creation and procreation, cannot co-exist in Mayne's stories as, indeed, they fail to in her novels.[5] Mayne's critical examination of gender roles and the Victorian idealisation of motherhood participates in the larger debate about the "Woman Question" at the *fin de siècle*. In their exploration of gendered norms, male-female relations and female creativity, the stories from *The Clearer Vision* thus reflect the concerns raised by other New Woman writers at the time (Pykett 1992, 137ff.; Ledger 1997). Adela's very outspoken rejection of "the fetish", as she ironically calls the hallowed maternal instinct, can also be read as a direct response to the celebration of motherhood as a source of female empowerment by writers such as Sarah Grand and George Egerton (O'Toole 2013, 90–2). While Grand's short fiction often promotes motherhood as the source of a larger social justice, Egerton calls "the maternal instinct" "the *only divine* fibre in a woman", even if, in her more utopian stories, motherhood does not exclude the possibility of authorship (Fluhr, 2001, 255–256; Egerton 2006, 108). As Mayne's daughter stories in *Blindman* and *Come In* show, Mayne herself is more sceptical of innate maternal feelings; she is also far more critical of actual mothers than her fellow New Woman writers (D'hoker 2020, 149–151).

That Mayne, like many other New Woman writers, turned to the genre of the modern short story to express these proto-feminist concerns can be explained, in part, by the energy and popularity that surrounded the form in the 1890s. Moreover, the periodical boom made it possible for many more writers, including women, to make a living from their pen while literary magazines, like *The*

---

5. The talented pianist Millicent North, who may have been based on Mayne's mother (cf. supra), sacrifices her artistic ambitions for marriage in *One of Our Grandmothers* and, as *The Fourth Ship* shows, rather unhappily submits to a domestic life as wife and mother. The tension between creativity and procreation, between art and life, was often explored in late-nineteenth-century fiction, by male and female, aestheticist and naturalist (or new realist) writers (D'hoker 2017).

Yellow Book and *Chapman's Magazine*, welcomed stories by women writers. At the same time, the genre's novelty seemed to allow for a greater freedom to experiment, not just with literary techniques, but also with alternative narrative patterns and plots. Indeed, in Mayne's early stories, as in the short fiction of writers like Grand, D'Arcy, Egerton and Netta Syrett, formal experimentation goes hand in hand with a questioning of Victorian gendered norms. The still flexible genre of the short story clearly proved useful to these women writers for evading the strictures of the marriage plot that dominated the novel (D'hoker and Eggermont 2015, 298–301). In the stories from *The Clearer Vision* too, fragmentation and impressionism serve to challenge the inevitability of marriage for young women and to question the social codes that underpin this expectation.

In this combination of formal experimentation with New Woman concerns, *The Clearer Vision* recalls in particular Egerton's *Keynotes*. Ellipsis, impressionism and fragmentation are notable characteristics of Egerton's stories as well (D'hoker 2016, 26–9). Moreover, both collections reveal the influence of such *fin-de-siècle* movements as aestheticism, symbolism and naturalism. Like Egerton, Mayne likes to use symbols and images from other art forms—music, poetry, painting—in her stories. "On the Programme", for instance, is structured around the different dances at a ball—"Pas-de-quatre", "Kitchen Lancers" and "Valse"—and artists and writers are recurring figures throughout her first collection. Like Egerton's stories in *Keynotes,* moreover, Mayne's early stories seek to establish their literary credentials through references to other writers, from Byron, Tennyson and Browning to Nietzsche, Anatole France and Alphonse Daudet. Finally, Egerton's oft-quoted ambition of wanting to document "the terra incognita of herself, as she knew herself to be, not as man liked to imagine her" also applies to Mayne's stories (Egerton 1932, 58). Indeed, Egerton and Mayne are primarily interested in recording the complex inner lives of their female characters.

Where the two writers differ, however, is in their characterisation of this "terra incognita". If for Egerton, women's inner lives seem primarily grounded in the body and driven by desire, Mayne's female protagonists are more cerebral. They self-reflexively scrutinize their own thoughts and feelings, critically comparing them to the social norm. Moreover, while Egerton often alludes to woman's "true nature" which is being distorted by artificial gendered conventions, there is no such essential womanhood in Mayne's stories. Instead, Mayne foregrounds her characters' self-conscious performance of normative femininity, which is ambivalently valued as playful and restricting at the same time.

Anglo-Irish Stories

Apart from a shared interest in the short story, affiliation with *The Yellow Book* and desire to document women's inner lives, Mayne and Egerton also have in common an Irish background. Like Mayne, Egerton wrote her first story collection in County Cork even though *Keynotes*, like *The Clearer Vision*, lacks any overt reference to Ireland. Both writers, however, would return to Irish settings and Irish characters in subsequent story collections. Yet, for all these similarities, the Irish worlds depicted by Egerton and Mayne are quite far apart. While Egerton directs her arrows primarily at the snobbery and materialism of the Catholic, Dublin middle class she grew up in, Mayne's Ireland is that of the Anglo-Irish Protestant gentry, living on small estates in provincial garrison towns.[6]

---

6. While Mayne's family is certainly Protestant, her mother's family did have Catholic ancestors, much like Millicent North in *One of Our Grandmothers* and the Burke family in "The Turret-Room". In a letter of 6 August 1924 to Macgillivray, Mayne explains about her religious affiliations as follows: "All [my mother's] people had been Catholics, but her father [con]verted to marry her mother (a Miss Button) and so she was a Protestant; but when she was dying, she had a wish, which, of course, could not be granted, to see a priest instead of her clergyman. The priest would not have come to her—the clergyman did, and

Mayne had relocated to London by the time she was writing her second collection, *Things That No One Tells*; nonetheless, most of its stories are either set in Ireland or feature Irish characters abroad. Although these stories return to the themes explored in *The Clearer Vision*—male-female relationships, social conventions and female consciousness—the Irish inflection brings to these themes a more precisely observed social context as well as a greater depth of feeling. At the same time, the Irish context also invariably seems to worsen the already unenviable situation of Mayne's genteel young ladies. In "Photographs" and "The Boulevardiers", for instance, the young girls are as preoccupied with attracting and negotiating male attention in the marriage market as the English girls in *The Clearer Vision*, yet the greater insularity of their provincial Irish context and the dearth of sophisticated intellectual society makes their preoccupation at once more vulgar and more hopeless. This is suggested in both stories by a juxtaposition with more widely travelled characters: the Malet sisters in "Photographs" who have "the mark of the nomad [...] upon them" (p.65 in this volume) and the young Frenchmen in "The Boulevardiers" who make fun of the silly naiveté of the Irish girls. At the same time, however, the stories also point at the more fundamental similarities underlying these oppositions: Sylvia Malet ruefully admits that she has "'his photo', just like them" (p.72 in this volume) and in "The Boulevardiers", the Dublin girls' more worldly father, the Colonel, is also only interested in chatting up a French saleswoman.

If the limitations of parochial Irish society are satirically exposed in these stories, they receive a more tragic realisation in "Desertsurges" from the same collection. Its opening description

---

I have never in all my life seen or heard anything so frightfully inadequate as he was—for she kept me with her, as though she were afraid of that very thing. My elder brother has become a Catholic, and my younger brother has married one! Strangely enough, when there was already something of it in the blood—or rather, I suppose, not strangely at all. Like you, I am not of the Western Churches; but <u>not</u> like you, I don't find anything to look to in Buddhism."

of the Irish country house of the title—"gloomy", "ugly", "dull", at the end of a "long, dark avenue" (p.80 in this volume)—aptly sets the stage for the Big House drama that will unfold. The two Bolton sisters who live in the house, together with their domineering aunt and hapless uncle, also recall the trappings of the Big House genre, familiar from the novels of George Moore, Somerville and Ross and, later, Elizabeth Bowen. Like many Big House heroines, the girls feel "trapped" within the house and the limited circumstances of their class (Kreilkamp 1998, 23).[7] While the elder, more serious sister appears to accept her fate, the younger sister is ready to elope with a married man. What Mayne adds to these themes is an exploration of the studied performance of gendered roles which both the girl and her suitor indulge in. The girl's performance of conventional female modesty receives a darker edge, however, when it turns out to hide not just a more worldly knowledge and sexual passion (as in Egerton's stories), but a more profound naiveté about the bleakness of her fate within a defunct social order. The story aptly underlines the hopelessness of her position through the isolation and strange otherworldliness of the Anglo-Irish Big House and through the sarcastic predictions of the Irish gatekeeper: "'Tis old maids they'll be, the two of them, I tell ye this night. Divil a young gentleman comes next or nigh the place; 'tmight as well call itself a convent and be done with it" (p.95 in this volume).

Even though there is no shortage of young men in "The Turret-Room", the downfall of the Big House and the social order it represents is even more graphically represented in this story from Mayne's third collection, *Come In*. In this story too, the daughters fall into two opposed types: Nellie, the more serious and plain elder sister is juxtaposed to her more beautiful sisters who pass the time by flirting with the "the gay, the transient soldiers, or the still more gay and transient sailors" (p.103 in this volume)

---

7. For a more extensive discussion of these "Big House" stories, see D'hoker 2020, 143–154.

the garrison town supplies in endless rotation. Nellie's sense of entrapment within the decaying world of the Big House is symbolised by the turret-room of the title, with its stuck door, whose only redeeming feature is a view of the river. The burning of the Big House in "The Turret-Room" is another familiar trope of Big House fiction, which is given an almost surreal twist through the burial of Nellie's ashes together with those of the house she could not escape.[8] As in "Desertsurges", moreover, the tragic fate of Nellie—and the other daughters of the Big House—is given extra poignancy through the laconic commentary of the servants and the traditional keening of the local women. In short, these stories, set in rural or small-town Ireland, clearly participate in a tradition of Anglo-Irish fiction that stretches back to Maria Edgeworth and that would lead on to Elizabeth Bowen, Molly Keane and Jennifer Johnston. Mayne is original, however, in her choice of the short story to capture these Big House themes that have far more often been the province of the novel. By rendering the sad plight of Anglo-Irish daughters through only a few well-chosen scenes, the stories compellingly bring out the stasis of their lives which can only end in death: either the violent death by fire of "The Turret-Room" or the slow death of the empty spinster's life predicted in "Desertsurges".

When Mayne revisits the restricted lives of Anglo-Irish daughters in subsequent collections, the Big House tropes have been left behind for a greater focus on mother-daughter relationships. The capricious and repressive aunt in "Desertsurges", whom the Bolton sisters try to keep in a good mood, resurfaces as the domineering mother in such stories as "The Separate Room", "The Letter on the Floor", "The Peacocks" and "Light". As I have argued

---

8. The story was inspired by the burning of Menlo Castle, home of the Blake family, in Galway in July 1910. It was reported that the body of the family's invalid eldest daughter, Eleanor (born, like Mayne, in 1865), was never found among the ruins of the castle. I am grateful to Susan Waterman for alerting me to this source of inspiration.

elsewhere, the mother in these stories "is represented as a cruel, selfish, omnipotent figure, whose dominion limits the daughter's growth and corrodes her sense of self" (D'hoker 2020, 149–151). Mayne's "devouring mothers" thus participate in a long tradition of suffocating mother-daughter bonds in Irish women's fiction (Fogarty 2002; Ingman 2007, 67–95). Mayne's treatment of this theme in a series of short stories, however, adds to this tradition an interesting sense of development, whereby the daughter gradually achieves a better understanding of the mother's position. In all four stories, the mother's vindictive anger is sparked in particular by her daughter's increasing independence, whether in terms of professional achievement, artistic ambition or love life. Since the mother's reprisals alternate with great shows of motherly affection, the daughters in these stories can be seen to try—and fail—to separate performance from reality. While the gruesome ending of "The Separate Room" prevents a mother-daughter reconciliation, the daughter in "The Letter on the Floor" comes to realise that her mother's anger may well originate in her own frustrated confinement in marriage, motherhood and those nineteenth-century gender roles which her daughter seems poised to leave behind. In "The Peacocks" and "Light", finally, the daughter looks back with a greater sense of resignation on her fraught relationship with her mother, after the latter's death and from the vantage-point of her own independent life in London.[9]

Modernism and Modernity

That the protagonist from "The Peacocks" managed to escape from the gloomy fate of the spinster predicted for her in Ireland may testify to the greater opportunities available for women in London, which Mayne herself experienced. Yet it also points to

---

9. Nicola Beauman briefly discusses the depiction of mother-daughter relations in "Light" in *A Very Great Profession: The Woman's Novel 1914–39* (2008, 224–5).

the way Mayne's stories from the 1910s and 1920s bear witness to the changes that the first-wave feminist movement had wrought in women's lives and gender norms. If in "The Separate Room" and "The Letter on the Floor", the protagonists' brief stints as "working women" are frowned upon by their elders, in "The Man of the House", the three Miss Mounts all had to learn a trade at the insistence of their provident father. In an endearing little scene, Mayne highlights the difference this makes, as the sisters recognise, "[y]ou weren't old maids when you were business-women" and "[o]ld maids are failures; we aren't failures" (p.135 in this volume). In this way, the story can also be read as an interesting counterpoint to Katherine Mansfield's "The Daughters of the Late Colonel" (1920), where the death of an authoritarian father leaves his two genteel daughters utterly helpless, impoverished and bereft.

The comparison with Mansfield can also be extended to the narrative techniques of Mayne's later stories. In *The Clearer Vision*, the characters' complex inner lives were typically evoked through long passages of (free) indirect thought, while in "The Man of the House", the personality of the Mount sisters is revealed through their reactions to a central incident, the sudden illness and death of their cat. In a similar way, the relationship between the two newly-weds in "The Happy Day" is revealed through their visit to Galway, rather than speculatively dissected from the perspective of a bemused outsider as was the case in "One Near One". The greater unity and condensation which Mayne is able to achieve in these later stories reflects the development from the experimental proto-modernist poetics of *The Yellow Book* writers to the mature modernism of writers like Mansfield and Bowen. In her narratological analysis of the modernist short story, indeed, Sabine Buchholz discusses Mayne's "Stripes" alongside Bowen's "Lunch", Woolf's "Mrs Dalloway in Bond Street" and Mansfield's "At the Bay" to show how the modernist story succeeds in plumbing psychological depth through the description of entirely ordinary experiences (Buchholz 2003, 128–9). In Mayne's story, a young woman tries to sell a striped blouse at a jumble sale, speculating about the (unhappy) relationship of prospective clients, while also reminiscing about the end of her own betrothal some years earlier.

Mayne's bridging of the gap between *fin-de-siècle* Aestheticism and early-twentieth-century modernism makes her unique in the history of the modern short story. With regard to Irish short fiction in particular, her work thus constitutes the missing link between the avant-garde, experimental stories of George Egerton and the late modernist short fiction of Elizabeth Bowen and Norah Hoult. Mayne's penultimate story collection, *Nine of Hearts*, was published in the same year as Bowen's first volume, *Encounters* (1923), and Mayne knew both writers and their work.[10] With Bowen's more "popular" or "middlebrow" modernist short fiction (Hunter 2007, 112; D'hoker 2016, 53–5), Mayne's later stories share a greater generic diversity, as the impressionist, plotless story, defended by James and Harland, comes to be combined with the plots of such popular genres as the crime story, the melodrama or the thriller. "Gytha Wellwood" and "The Shirt of Nessus", for instance, revolve around murder and the descent into madness. The latter story is particularly chilling because it is told from the perspective of the man whose mental breakdown gives expression to a deep hatred of women. "The Angry Place", to give another example, displays the tropes of the horror story as nature suddenly turns threatening on an ordinary country walk. "A Hair of the Dog" takes on the theme of tourism from "The Happy Day", but turns it into a funny story, with a surprising twist at the end. Mayne also wrote some war stories, both during and after the First World War. The 1917 collection *Come In* contains an original take

---

10. Marcia Farrell lists Mayne as one of Bowen's correspondents and Bowen included a short story by Mayne, "The Man of the House", in her 1936 anthology, *The Faber Book of Modern Short Stories* (Farrell 2007: 397). Norah Hoult based a fictional character on Mayne in her novel *There Were No Windows*, which is a fictionalised account of the last years of Violet Hunt.

on shellshock, "Forgetfulness", while "Canneton à la Presse", from *Nine of Hearts*, tells of an Austrian chef who returns to his London restaurant after the war. "Franklin's Problem", the final story of Mayne's last collection, *Inner Circle*, is a story of adultery that recalls the adulterous affairs in Bowen's stories.

In her very last stories, however, Mayne returned to Ireland once again—not, this time, the Ireland of her young adulthood, which is depicted so damningly in *Things That No One Tells* and *Come In*, but the Ireland of her childhood in Kinsale, County Cork. "The Picnic" and "The Lower Road" revolve around an Anglo-Irish family in Kinsale: nine-year-old Rosamund, her younger sister Lottie, her parents, and their nanny Bridget. Both stories are told from the perspective of Rosamund and show her trying to make sense of the adult world around her. In "The Picnic" she gets lost during a family outing, worries that the local bogeyman, "Old Jacky", will get hold of her, and is dismayed by her parents' unconcerned reaction when she is found.[11] In "The Lower Road", Bridget finds their usual walking route cordoned off because of an outbreak of scarlet fever and decides to take the girls along the notorious Lower Road, where they spy a prostitute and a soldier in the field. Even though Rosamund doesn't understand what she has witnessed, she is intrigued and frightened by the adults' reactions and the "girl's red face stayed in Rosie's eyes all that day" (Mayne 1928, 253). Both stories cleverly conjure up an adult world through the girl's limited and naïve perspective, a narrative strategy that can also be found in Bowen's childhood stories.

In all, the greater variety and accomplishment of Mayne's final collections show the distance she has travelled from her early,

---

11. In a letter to Macgillivray, 13 July 1924, Mayne suggests that the story was based on a childhood memory: "It was lovely to get the wild roses—oddly enough, I was just then working at a story which is full of them. It tells about myself as a little child, when I got lost, or thought I had, upon the old Head of Kinsale. Lots of 'my sort of stuff' in it—lots, at least, that I remember as vividly as if it had happened yesterday, and therefore assume that other children would have felt too."

proto-modernist New Woman stories. Nevertheless, the entire range of her short fiction—in terms of time as well as of thematic scope—demands that we recognise Mayne as a significant voice in British and Irish literature. The selection of short stories presented in this book should help to give a first impression of Mayne's distinctive achievements in the genre.

A Note on the Selected Stories

The short stories in this volume span Mayne's six short story collections. "The End of It" and "Lucille" come from *The Clearer Vision*, but earlier versions of these stories were published in *The Yellow Book*. "Photographs", "The Boulevardiers" and "Desertsurges" were taken from Mayne's second collection, *Things That No One Tells*. "The Turret-Room" was published in *Come In* and "The Happy Day", "The Man of the House" and "The Letter on the Floor" in *Blindman*. Finally, "The Peacocks" and "The Picnic" are from *Nine of Hearts* and *Inner Circle*, respectively. For the sake of reference, the tables of contents of all collections are given below with the stories included here indicated in bold. I have selected these particular stories because they are representative of Mayne's central concerns as well as of the formal developments of her short fiction. Given the focus of this book series, I have prioritised stories that are set in Ireland or stage Irish characters. This volume does not contain all her "Irish" stories, however, nor do all the selected stories sport such an explicit Irish dimension. In my selection I have also been guided by my own predilections and preferences. Yet there are many more fascinating and complex stories which could have made it into this collection were it not for restrictions of space. It is to be hoped that they will find their way to readers by other means. Save for correcting a few typographical errors, I have not made any changes to the texts, which retain their original punctuation, abbreviations, occasional archaisms and variant spellings to indicate dialect.

The Clearer Vision (1898): "Herb of Grace", **"Lucille"**, **"The End of It"**, "The Lost Leader", "On the Programme", "One Near One", "Ritournelle".

Things That No One Tells (1910): "The Red Umbrella", **"Desertsurges"**, "Violets Pluckt", **"The Boulevardiers"**, "Embassies Delayed", "The Bungalow", "Madeline Annesley", "Blue Muslin", **"Photographs"**, "The One Way" and "Honoria Byron".

Come In (1917): "The Separate Room", "Four Ballrooms", "Lovells Meeting", "The Kingfisher", "Three Rooms", "Forgetfulness", **"The Turret-Room"**.

Blindman (1919): **"The Letter on the Floor"**, **"The Happy Day"**, "A Dab at Human Nature", "The Angry Place", "Christina", "A Hair of the Dog", "Grey's Impressions", "Reassurance", **"The Man of the House"**.

Nine of Hearts (1923): "Gytha Wellwood", "Canneton à la Presse", "Silver Paper", "Smaragdov", "Interlude for Death", "Gold Hair", "India-rubber", **"The Peacocks"**, "Light".

Inner Circle (1925): "The Latchkey", "The Shirt of Nessus", "Black Magic", "Stripes", "White Hair", "Campaign", "Lavender and Lucinda", **"The Picnic"**, "Still Life", "Dialogue in a Cab", "Franklin's Problem".

The Stories

The End of It (*The Clearer Vision*, 1898)

I
THE ESCAPE

"It is better to fall into the hands of a murderer, than into the dreams of an ardent woman."—*Nietzsche*[1]

They were going away on the morrow, she and her father, so that this would be the last of the little dinners—the quaint, sudden little dinners that had been "happening" so often of late. To-night they had invited him; but how many times had he not dumbly invited himself! Invited? that was a shred-like way of expressing it. She would come in from a picnic, or a day on the river, sometimes even—so entirely without warning to either of them would it happen—from a long drive into the country with her father; and on the round table of their lodging-house room, they would see that instead of their own demure two places, three were laid.

---

1. The quote is from *Thus Spake Zarathustra*, which was first translated into English by Alexander Tille in 1896. Yet, Tille translates the phrase as "Is it not better to fall into the hands of a murderer than into the dreams of a lustful woman" (Nietzsche 1896, 71). Mayne may have read the book in German and made her own translation, or she may have taken the quote from Havelock Ellis' 1896 article on Nietzsche in *The Savoy*, which uses this exact same phrase (Ellis 1896, 83).

"Hullo!" her father would say, half-amused, half-satirical.

She would say nothing, as a rule, but sometimes she would laugh, and pretend that she thought it rather impertinent.

"It's always *he* who dines with us!" she would cry. "Oh yes! I know that we 'combine forces,' as he says—but can't he ask us down to his room, occasionally?"

"Catch Luttrell doing that! It is Luttrell?"

"Of course it is Luttrell. Look at the small knife and fork; you know he 'can't see what large knives and forks are *for*!'"

She would mimic, with the almost involuntary mimicry of great liking, a somewhat harsh, dragging, yet pleasant and intensely high-bred voice.

And then she would dress in a simulated "hurry," knowing all the while that she could not for her life have done anything slowly when Luttrell was coming, in that eccentric way of his, to dine with them.

But to-night's was the last of these dear little three-cornered dinners; for they were going away on the morrow. Nothing quite like this could ever happen again, nothing so almost quaintly compact: she and her father, lodging in the same house with his brusque, fascinating, gentle, laughable Luttrell! who said so often, with that suggestion of satyr-like qualities which could invest him with an unacknowledged repulsiveness, that he "didn't like girls."

"So few men do!" she would sigh demonstratively; "don't be commonplace."

Then he would peer at her suspiciously, and she would feel that, in his language, she "had scored."

There was something rather excitingly intricate about her intercourse with him, she thought gaily. Her keen perception of it seemed to vivify even the most mechanical parts of the business of dressing. To stand before the complaisant looking-glass in a delicate blue dressing-gown, with a confusion of laces and ribbons underneath that testified to the daintiness of her *lingerie*, was doubly pleasant because she knew that his fastidious motto was:

You dress for yourself; and to see her dark hair framing her face for an instant, before it was brushed into the long lines that he had so often perplexedly praised: "How is it your hair looks so much more 'classy'" (the touching futility of his vocabulary!) "than the other girls'?"—that was delightful, too! There was an esoteric pleasure in the thought that he could not imagine how nice she looked with her hair down—a sense of plenitude, of having something in excess of what he already found so attractive.

He was insistently, however, her father's friend; the two men were not very far removed in age. But she—more intensely, humorously conscious and observant of him than any one could have guessed from the singular *naïveté* of her almost adoring manner—she had, every time he came, the sly delicate satisfaction of watching his gradually widening detachment from anything, on those evenings, which did not concern her: a detachment that she knew he quite genuinely explained to himself as a kind of patronizing, elderly perception of her uncalculated charm.

Yes; there was, in many ways, something delightfully intricate about their intercourse, she thought again, swinging open the glass door of the wardrobe to choose her gown. The fragrance which came towards her on the abrupt passage of air was another subtle personal flattery. It was a mixture of the perfumes which had been associated with the various frocks. One had always had moss-roses for its accompanying cluster, and the sweet, slender smell of the faded buds still breathed from the white satin, the rosy chiffon and silver embroidery: another, of amber silk and grey-blue mistiness, she had worn with violets—there swept from those folds the clear, fine, impetuous odour, with its inexplicable suggestion of the sea; some, less receptive, had merely the scent of their original materials—the crisp, thin modishness of tulle, the luxurious smugness of velvet....

She chose finally the most fragrant and delicate of them all—one in white and clear, pale blue, that wafted, hesitatingly, jessamine and stephanotis. Quite absurd to wear it to-night!—but it was the last time, one might as well look nice. She tossed the skirt over her head, then let it trail, unfastened, from her waist, while she hooked the invisibly-secured bodice, whose complications were made still more perplexing by the frills of chiffon that hung down, catching perpetually, with a frail drifting persistence, and ravelling themselves, upon the skin of even her fine, smooth fingers. She tucked some of them into the opening, and held the longer ones under her chin—looking into the glass with amused, critical eyes, to see how she was, like that.

It was such fun, all this pretending—these airs and graces, these sudden, premeditated fits of absence of mind, these deprecations, these humilities! Sometimes, during dessert, if by chance the two men *did* wander to the club-gossip which he talked so heedlessly ("before a woman!" she used to say, with a teasing, flattered glance), she would rise, with a little suggestion of being, she supposed, "in the way;" and would go to the far end of the long, narrow room. How soon there would be a movement at the table, the pushing back of a chair, a sauntering footstep in her direction! She was always, then, aware of some inexplicable irritation, almost a physical shiver, as though a moth or a fly were crawlingly teasing her. But this she put aside as a thing of small significance; or, if she did ponder it, explained it as the natural half-amused exasperation of every woman with the amazing crudity of mankind. One would have thought her little device so transparent: what was the use of women's being at all subtle or *rusées* when it only needed an obviousness like that!

She wondered—pulling the frills at last from their hiding-place, and tossing them into shape with the back of her hand— what it was that she really did feel for Luttrell. He, in the meek reserve of the antiquated phrase, "occupied her thoughts." That was supposed to be a synonym for being the man with whom one was ready to fall in love. Was she, then, ready—what absurdity! we were at the end of the century!—was she *in love* with Luttrell?

Her great grey eyes, gleaming like dark crystals with excitement, the vivid, tender flush in her cheeks, her lips that had taken a droll little curl, actually almost imperceptible, yet powerfully modifying in its tiny effect—which her brothers called, "Effie's crooked mouth, a certain sign of her being excited!"—all this outward exaltation might well have availed to answer her.

But she was aware that it did not answer her. Hers was a curious perversity of idealisation. In her unremitting study of him, there was so essential an aloofness of vanity—could love be this clever? That was unimaginable, and, to her, repellent also; for she had an ideal of herself "in love," which she knew, even while almost passionately she cherished it, was that of a woman who is foredoomed to failure. She divined, in a word, that hers was the fatal lack of reserve in ardent feeling; that, far from playing with the man whom she could love, as she played with Luttrell, she would, on the contrary, find the most striking proof of his admiration almost an incredibility. And yet for her to attract any one who did not value these ingenuities, these coquetries, was the most unlikely of unlikelihoods. It was, invariably, through them that she prevailed. But she could not dimly conceive herself practicing them upon the lover of her unwilling dreams! It seemed a sort of *impasse*, and one from which an issue might not be indispensable.

"*Ça fait toujours plaisir!*" she sang softly, radiant at last in her cloud-like blue and white. How well she was looking! how right to have chosen this gown! Moving from the toilet-table to the long cheval-glass, she took triumphantly the *coup d'œil*, from the dark hair, with its sparkle of tiny diamonds, down by the graceful bodice, the narrow silver belt, the crisp lissom skirt, to the black silk stocking and shoe with its paste-buckle which she had thought full-dress enough for so small an occasion. And, besides, the shoes were so pretty, the stockings so becomingly open-worked! One could see *that* very clearly under the foam of lace-edges. "*You dress for yourself.*" She put at once a charming affirmation, and a question-mark, to his sumptuary motto, as she turned quickly at the sound of his voice downstairs, and went to the toilet-table to blow out the candles.

Even their acrid fumes could not overcome the fragrance that drifted through the half-open door, as Luttrell, a few seconds later, passed it on his way to the sitting-room.

There was a comical mixture of elements at these dinners. They went their jerking lodging-house way, amid Luttrell's odd, talkative languor and her own intense consciousness of spontaneity; while her father's amused, half-ironical indulgence supplied the last elaboration—the sense of an audience, of a final arbitrator; for there was the further anomaly in their intercourse that a tête-à-tête was the least of their mutual pleasures.

The quaintness of it all seemed typified by the *décor* of the meetings, the combination of elegance and an almost countrified roughness: the exquisite flowers—pink tulips and asparagus-fern in delicate grey-green vases—under the heavy, shapeless lamp with its crimped-paper shade; the pretty, awkward maid who poked the dishes between the gay whispering of the champagne in their glasses; Luttrell, with his ineffable distinction—the look of being sharply cut out of the air—and the absurd directions he would drawl out to the agonized Nora!

It was wholly unique, delightful, not to be had again; and though better things might well be in the future, there would be none with just this intimate, ephemeral charm. For of course it could not have lasted like this, was bound to have ended speedily in one way or another.

One way or another! There was one way in which it had no likelihood of ending—and that the way in which almost every one might have looked for it to end. For Luttrell to wish to marry her was the wildest improbability: there were a hundred reasons against it; and yet, to-night, there was a something, a veiled regret, a hinted revolt against circumstance....

"God help any girl who ever cares a red cent about me!" he had said, almost impetuously, in his curiously ineffective slang. They had been talking, with insincerity that the moment seemed clumsily to force upon them, of ideals.

"You've got past that stage?" he said, with a nervous, self-conscious cynicism; "have guessed how dull it would be to meet your ideal?"

"I don't believe in having one, till I do meet him," she answered.

"Oh, that's very easy. Any one will do for that," he drawled, audaciously; "even *I* might."

"You don't see what I mean. It's quite the other way round. What I think is—if you have your ready-made ideal, it's the easiest thing in the world to read him into any one at all charming. Whereas, if you haven't! The delight of finding him out, new, every day! and *there* for you to talk to, and —"

"And?" The satyr-like look crept into the heavy-lidded eyes, and lost him the answer he expected.

"And—find dull!" she nodded to him. "Ideals are wearisome dear things. It's so much more interesting to like what one really doesn't in the least approve of."

"I'm afraid I can't follow you," he said, annoyed; "these wildnesses of yours—I don't approve of *them*."

"Ah! perhaps I'm your ideal; and you'll only find it out—the day after to-morrow." Her sigh was quite spontaneous. But he grew angry at the audacity; it seemed to his uneasy, elderly vanity that she ought not to have been capable of it. When girls *cared*! He had certainly thought that she did. His face fell a little, looked coarser in grain, more animal.

"I shall write and tell you," he said, with an edge of insolence upon the thin drawl, and he stretched his hand for the champagne-bottle.

"Oh, pen-and-ink!" she cried lightly, "a pen-and-ink effect! It's so utterly *en l'air* –"

"I hate your French phrases," he muttered sulkily.

"In the air," she translated; "in the air of the new place, the new people, the new—ideals." Her voice dropped cleverly on the last word.

"But it's not a new place, Effie," said her father. "We've been there before, you know."

"Yes; in the dark ages, when I was going to school. Is there anything more crushing to your retrospective vanity than meeting your pet school-friends of—all those years ago, and seeing how they strike you now? One wants to believe one was always a person of discrimination."

"Ideals again!" Luttrell clung to the word, as though he wanted to say something in especial. It found expression at last. "Ideals! I hope I was never anybody's." And then, he had made that impulsive speech: "God help any girl who ever cares a red cent about me!"

There was something galling about it—about the suggestion of warning in this emotional depreciation of himself; yet there was, too, something that was a little touching. She felt for the first time a thrill of genuine tenderness; it seemed as though one might have loved him, have lost the self-consciousness and the vanity, have found in him something of the difficult hero of one's dreams ... But Luttrell! Every one knew that Luttrell was already more than half-pledged, was far more than half-infatuated. It would be folly to measure herself against a social inferior in a contest that she would not win; and yet—there was a tone in the voice, a look on the weary, cryptic, cynical face....

She left the table in her light, irresponsible way.

"Time for the hour of bereavement," she said. "You see I say it in English. But could any one mistake it for an English sentiment?"

"No. *We* say, the hour of relievement," he retorted, sending her from under shadowing fingers a glance which contradicted his words.

But she seated herself in the distant window with an air of aloofness. In that moment, she felt the sudden, unreasoning, almost vacuous weariness with it all that sometimes swept over like a mist-wreath. It was as if she could not talk any more, could not smile and glance any longer. What was it that one needed so achingly? what made one thus suddenly drift away from all self-possession, all consciousness nearly, into a kind of confused helplessness? This man—fascinating in his perverse and kindly cynicism—what was it in him that revolted her, irritated her sometimes to anger, when (as now) she saw him grow restless, absent-minded, push back his chair, come towards her? The odd physical shiver ran through her nerves; yet, even while she almost petulantly questioned herself, she felt again the faint thrill that had come when he said he hoped he was nobody's ideal. She looked at him coldly, as he drew nearer, and the deprecating glance he gave her, as though he doubted his welcome, made her heart beat a little faster. After all, should she try, seriously try? For, deep down in her consciousness, she divined that she could move him, delicately, graciously, with a fine ardour, as—it was inconceivable that the other woman could do! It was worth trying!

And, while the hours went by in desultory talk and short, significant silences, her heart drew out towards him almost tenderly. He was very lovable, he was worthy of something a little better than what it seemed he was drifting to. For, still with that curious new impulsiveness, he told them—in hints and broken phrases, in looks and silences—of what was likely to happen. She felt sorry that things had turned out so; that to-night, when the little comedy was at its last scene, she should have recognized a possibility of something more real than they had touched hitherto. Vanity might still be the motive-power; but in how different an aspect! an almost spiritual aspect—was it?

The starlight gleamed through the open window upon the soft answering shimmer of satin, the flash of the little diamond combs, of the dark, crystal-like eyes; upon the silver fittings of her father's pipe, the cut-glass bottle of whiskey on the round lacquered table; upon Luttrell's gold studs and cufflinks, his soft, pallid, oddly undistinguished hands, the clear amber liquid in his glass, as he lifted it perpetually to his lips.

He was talking on, reminiscently now, with a sort of rough sadness, a queer cynical tenderness; speaking of a time when he had been in love with a married woman, had "dree'd his weird,"[2] had "made up his mind about a heap of things." Her father listened with a slight uneasiness; he was old-fashioned, thought "the line should be drawn before girls"—but Luttrell was a privileged person: it was only by an almost imperceptible twisting in his chair, a very rare darkening of his bright blue eyes, that he conveyed his disapproval. Her own interest had grown a little complicated, a little distracted even, for she wondered more and more as he talked, *what* was making him so almost sentimentally confidential this evening. It invested him with the last attraction. Was he telling her (it was "her," not "them!") all this as a sort of renunciation, a burying of his past? And then that subtly-hinted relinquishment of the hitherto probable future—did it mean that all was to be hers?

And if it were so?

Well, it would please her, make her happier than she could have believed before to-night. If Luttrell were, in the absurd phrase, to be "her fate?" It would be what she had dreamt of? Well, almost! and this evening, too, she had been conscious of having (delightfully) lost her pose a little, been less clever, less *rusée*. The *impasse*, it seemed, had not after all been an *impasse*; she was out of it—with Luttrell! The farewell to-morrow would be only for a time.

"One o'clock!" he cried in dismay, hastily finishing his glass of whiskey-and-water, "and I've just smoked my last cigarette. I must go; you're going to be horribly busy in the morning. Well—good-night! but I shall see you to-morrow." He came forward, with a curious indecision, and she rose slowly to say the unwelcome words.

"Good-night," she murmured, almost shyly; his own look was

---

2. To endure or to submit to one's fate. (*OED Online*)

so nervous, so unsteady! Then she pulled herself together. "Goodnight. I'm so sorry this is our last little dinner. It has all been so pleasant. You mustn't forget us, you mustn't for a long time dine with the next people who take these rooms. Good-night!"

She turned away slightly as he went to the door; then, self-possessed again for the moment, she followed to watch him and her father go downstairs: it had always been part of their little programme for her to call some last gay challenge after him as he disappeared.

But to-night, he lingered obstinately upon the landing outside their room; and as he stood there, leaning against the balusters, a new mood—a mocking, hateful mood—seemed to come over him. He took out his handkerchief, and applied it, in flourishing burlesque of farewell-sorrow, to his eyes. It was the jocularity that above all others she detested; a dozen times they had agreed, she and Luttrell, that it was the most underbred of pleasantries. And—he was playing it off upon her! What on earth was the meaning of it? She turned swiftly away, angry, utterly mystified, wounded exceedingly. She had hardly left the doorway when she heard him go hastily, stumblingly, down the stairs.

Her father came hurrying back, and found her standing, helplessly, in the middle of the room, pale from hurt, delicate feeling. He looked half-amused, half-disgusted.

"Poor fellow!" he said, tentatively.

"Why, poor?" she coldly asked.

"Oh, well—you know! He's always perfectly right in the head, as rational as possible—though he may get a little sentimental, as you saw; still, quite rational. It's his legs that go wrong —"

"But what do you mean?" she stammered.

"Why, Effie, didn't you see? that was why he wouldn't go downstairs while you were looking. He knew he couldn't quite manage it."

"What do you mean?" she asked again. There might be some mistake, it might be *that* her father meant.

"A very little goes to his head,—his legs, rather! It's one o'clock. Just a little 'sprung,' I'm afraid. You mustn't be too indignant; it's hardly his fault. I wouldn't have told you, if —"

She hurried, without answering him, from the room. But, after she had reached her own, she reflected; and, opening the door she said, as her father stopped on his way upstairs to call good-night: "I don't envy the future Mrs Luttrell. Ah, but I daresay she won't mind so very much. Poor old dear!"

Then she shut herself in again. Her room was still fresh and fragrant; an open window sent in a sense of cool darkness. The relief after the smoky air of the sitting-room! But how hurt, angry, vaguely degraded she felt—how miserable! And, if she did, was it any wonder? If she did?

Suddenly, the full perception of the scene swept over her—the significance, the drama of it...

Luttrell, wavering ridiculously over his undressing in the room below, wondered if she had been very angry with him. He *had* been rather hateful; but he could not otherwise have got away without her noticing that he had—somewhat overstepped the boundary; and he was sure that, as he had managed, she could not possibly have guessed at it. To-morrow, he could make some teasing allusion to his having wanted to see *how* she would take the detested pleasantry; and everything would be all right. He was genuinely grieved—for he was sure that it must have wounded her horribly—but it had been the only way to make his escape. And goodness only knew what a girl of her sort would have thought of—the other thing. To escape had been imperatively necessary. He *had* escaped; of that he was confident.

Were they still talking upstairs? He could have sworn that he had heard her father going to his quarters in the top storey—but no! she could not be alone; they must be lingering in the open window of her room. Well! he had thought that she was sorry to say good-bye, that she had felt deeply, poignantly, that flippant gesture of his, enough even to have worried a little over it. But bah! all women were alike; not one of them had a spark of real feeling. Yes; there *was* her father's room-door banging. But if she was alone, what on earth was the girl laughing at?

Even in his irritation and discomfort—it was such a crowded room, his; he seemed to be for ever knocking up against something—the infectious stifled merriment made him wish, vaguely, that he could join in the joke.

II
A PEN-AND-INK EFFECT[3]

He was writing a letter, and as his pen jerked over the paper, he smiled with a fatuous softness. She had betrayed herself so helplessly, had cared so much. And he? Well, yes, he had cared, too, a little; who could have been quite unresponsive to that impetuous inquiring tenderness, that ardent generous admiration? He remembered it all, with amused regretful vanity—the summer evenings by the window, the gay give-and-take of their talk, the graver moments when their eyes met, and hers spoke more eloquently than words. "Eager tell-tales of her mind"—how often he had quoted Matthew Arnold's line when he thought of her eyes! It might have been written for her; and when he had told her so, she had not been angry. Little goose! She ought to have been, of course—but he might say anything, he knew.

Well! they had been pretty days, those; "a fragrant memory"— she had taught him some of her phrases—and now they were over. Quite over! The involuntariness of his sigh pleased him, and the reluctance with which he took up his pen again seemed to complete the romance of the moment.

She knew already. That was certain; he had sent a telegram on his wedding-day, thinking it might not be quite so bad if she knew he had thought of her even then. And now he was writing. Not to

---

3. The second part of the story was published as a separate story in *The Yellow Book* in July 1895, but Mayne rewrote it slightly for inclusion in "The End of It".

her—dear, no! he had too much tact, knowledge of the world, for *that*, he hoped; but to her father. They had been "pals" (he was so much older than she, "quite fatherly," he used to say, delighting in her conscious look); so it was natural, quite natural, for him to write and tell her father how it had happened.

For in some ways it was a queer business, not quite what had been expected of him, and yet—what every one had expected. *That* he knew, and it galled him sorely. It was hardly a *mésalliance*, perhaps, but—a mistake? He felt that it might be called one; a horrid saying jingled in his ears: "There's no fool like an old fool"—and yet he had chosen it so, always guessed that it would end so. Romantic? No! There was the sting—not even romantic.

But she? Would she look at it in that way? Would she smile and think that he had made a mess of it, compare herself mentally—her fastidious high-bred self—with his bride, and—pity him? He moved restlessly. No, she wouldn't; he knew her better. She would mind—mind horribly. Her mouth would set itself, her eyes would look bright and pained; oh, she was brave enough, but she would be silent, sadder than one had ever seen her, and—envious? His smile grew broader. Poor little dear!

At least, his letter would be some comfort. He had finished it; now to read it over. Yes; all was admirably conveyed. The regret, the remembrance, the veiled messages to her, the (he rather liked this part), the hinted depreciation of his choice, the insinuated unhappiness and foreboding; and then, the allusion to "his wife." ... In fancy he heard the quick, sharp breath, saw the darkening of the blue eyes, the pain of the firm little mouth....

But, stop! perhaps she might not see it at all. Men didn't hand letters round. He must provide against that. It was written for her—she *must* see it. How should he manage? Ah, that was it! "Your daughter will help you to make out my scrawl," in a prominent postscript; that was clear enough. Now to post it.

The end of the little episode, so delicate, so transient! Men were rather brutal, weren't they? Well, when girls fell in love—

and were so charming!—It *was* a shame, though, he thought complacently—poor little dear! The letter slid into the box.

Everything was going on just the same—and he was married. But then she had always known it must end so; every one had known it. There were two sorts of knowing, though, she thought, drearily.

For even the absurd climax of the last evening had not sent her from him with indifference. She had been amazed, when next morning they met for the farewells, to find herself still interested and fascinated. That had seemed to answer for more depth in her feeling from him than she had at all supposed it possessed—if one could forgive that? And forget that one had laughed at him? So many things didn't seem to be true, that had always been impressed upon one! That assertion of ridicule's annihilation of love—was anything more likely, on the face of it, to be true? Yet it wasn't; for she could not be abnormal, exceptional (if anything was a certainty, that was!); and she had laughed, the night before, with real amusement, at Luttrell—it *had* been at Luttrell? But of course; at whom else?—then, in the morning—it was odd....

And, now, it all seemed so natural; even having no letter to expect when the post came in seemed quite natural, and that *had* been the roseate moment of the day. Did everything happen so? Browning's poignant question came into her head: "Does truth sound bitter, as one at first believes?" She used to imagine he had been wrong for once ("that omniscient Browning of yours"), but now that she knew....

How *was* it? She could laugh quite naturally, could read, and be interested in her book. Stay, though! Yesterday she had been reading a story in which the heroine had reminded her of herself; and had of course loved and been beloved. She had shut that book hastily, and had taken up a volume of essays; but soon she had re-opened it, and devoured those scenes with envious, aching eyes.

That was the day after the telegram had come. It had stung her a little, though it had pleased her, too. So even at that moment, he had thought of her; but how sure he had been! That galled her; and, besides, it seemed to proclaim it all to the curious eyes around her. They were her own people, and she loved them, and they, her; still, their eyes were curious. She caught stolen glances, interchange of looks, imagined them talking of her: "Does she mind?" "Not so much as I expected"; oh, the torturing *espionage* of family life. If she could but have been quite alone—

She recalled the scene of the telegram. From her bedroom window she had seen the telegraph boy, had thought nothing of it—telegrams were so frequent.

"Effie! Effie!"

First her youngest brother, wide-eyed, observant, when the room-door burst open; then her father, half-understanding, but innately unsympathetic for "love-affairs," gratified, too, at the remembrance of him, careless or unconscious of the intolerable under-meaning of the message. Something had told her what it was, what the pink scrawl contained; she had felt a burning rebellion, a hard hatred of somebody or something.

"A telegram? From whom?" Her voice was sharp and cold. "From Luttrell?" This was one of the things she loathed—that she called him "Luttrell," *tout court*; her morbid sense of humour saw the painful absurdity of it: to speak so of a man you cared for! Incredible! yet she did it. Was anything in life what you had once fancied it?

"From Luttrell?" Bravado had forced the name from her—and if it should not be from him? Even now she could feel again the lash of the stinging thought.

"Yes; from Luttrell. Funny fellow! fancy his thinking of sending it! Like to see it?"

She had taken it with a laugh at the "funny fellow," had read it.

"So he's really married, you see, Effie. Well, she's a pretty girl, and a clever girl; I daresay he'll be very happy. An uncommonly clever girl."

How often, in her wayward moment, she had laughed with Luttrell over the "canonisation" of the newest *fiancée* or bride! "She has fulfilled the whole duty, the whole pleasure of woman!" she used to declaim with ironic grandiosity, while he smiled admiringly at her spirited nonsense. And now, it was he himself! But she must say something.

"Yes, she's pretty. Clever? Well, I never had the pleasure of her acquaintance." The tiny thrust had relieved her a little. "And where do they go for their honeymoon, I wonder?"

It was said: "they," "their honeymoon." Had her voice really sounded so thin and cold? She had felt just like it, "thin and cold," a meagre, desolate sort of creature. "Meagre!" how descriptive! Her lips curled into a small morbid smile; she remembered so well the odd sensation.

Well, that was over—two days ago, now—and she was going to lunch in that curious, dreamy sort of way, as though she were walking on air: everything was so natural, yet so unreal.

"The post just in? What letters?" she asked carelessly, passing through the hall.

"One from Luttrell."

"Why, Effie, Luttrell doesn't seem absorbed in his bride," her eldest brother said, reading his own letters. "Strikes me he'd rather have—"

She could have struck him—but this must be answered in his own vein. Would it never end? "Bored on the honeymoon, I suppose; they say every one is."

"*He* wouldn't be, though of course he'd pretend he was," her father laughed, opening the envelope; good heavens, what a scrawl! I can't read it. Here, Effie, you read it out; there's a postscript about you."

"No, indeed. I can't bear reading things aloud."

"Well, *I* can't. Take it, and read it to yourself, then?"

"I don't care about seeing it—as yet, at any rate. I'm hungry, for one thing. Can't it wait?"

"You know you're dying to see it," one of the brothers said, mockingly; "you'd both read it at the same time. Over his shoulder, Effie."

Well, if it had to be done.... She stood and read it over her father's shoulder.

It was long, illegible; she spelt it out slowly to her wondering, faltering heart. This was what he had written—this?

"A nice letter, very friendly. Poor old chap! Eh, Effie?"

"Yes, very—nice, very—friendly." She escaped.

In her room at last. "He wrote that? *That*?"

Her eyes met the wide dark ones in the mirror.

"Poor girl! oh, the poor, poor girl!" The mirror looked clouded, vanished quite, grew clear again. "To think I could ever have loved him!" For a moment she hid her shamed, white face.

"Feel up for a game of tennis, Ronald, Sydney, Edith!" her voice pealed out. One must do something to work off this mad joyous thrill of freedom, liberty ... looking forward!

She dashed down the stairs with a wild whirl of frills and lace-edges.

Lucille[4] (*The Clearer Vision*, 1898)

I can hardly expect you to understand me, I fear—for, if the truth be told, I understand myself not at all; and of Lucille, my comprehension is, at best, just not misapprehension: though of that, even, I feel at times uncertain enough.

Well, after this morning, I suppose I need not think about it any more. Need not! *must* not would express it better: the last word, so far as I am concerned in it, has been said; the curtain has rung down upon the little comedy-tragedy that I had (I might say) written, or, at any rate, conceived, entirely by and for myself; and it has left me—the author!—in a puzzlement that is,

---

4. "Lucille" was first published as the second part of Mayne's "Two Stories", which appeared in *The Yellow Book* in January 1896.

to treat it lightly, extremely disconcerting. I can't help having the preposterous feeling that it is partly my fault, its having ended so; and of course, you know, it isn't, couldn't be!

If we *will* take our drama in real life, we must not expect the unexpected, we must—strenuously—remember that we are author and audience both, that we see the thing from the inside, that we must be prepared for things actually happening, just as they seem to be going to happen.

I suppose I thought I had thus reasoned it all out, but I see now that my vision was irrevocably warped, that I was looking out, with a playgoer's certainty of anticipation, for the unprepared-for, the unexpected. But (I meant to have said sooner) it occurs to me that if I put it into words for you, if I reduce it, so to speak, to black and white, we may contrive between us to come to some sort of an understanding about it, to unravel at least one or two of the threads, to get in short an approximate idea of that slender humorous enigma whom we used to call Lucille Silverdale.

So now, if you are not alarmed at, repelled by, the prospect of a riddle, a puzzle—oh, but a very charming puzzle in brown hair and hazel eyes and sensitive contours?

Mrs. Silverdale, if she did not openly bemoan her fate, yet intimated tolerably plainly her resentment at the trick which Nature had played upon her; and, far from in sympathy though I felt with her, I could not deny that, from her point of view, there might be an excuse for her attitude. Her attitude? But, in truth, that is hardly the word; it was more a resigned recognition that there was no possible attitude to be taken up, a kind of mental huddle, a backboneless disapproval, an appallingly silent silence.

From the culprit herself, little aggression could be complained of; Lucille was, perhaps, as much ashamed of her inconvenience, her *inconvenance*, as were the most robust-minded of her family; but (it seemed to me) this very modesty, this very agreement with their envisagement of the situation, did but add an irritation the more to her personality.

Strange enough it was, too; one is used to see it taken so differently, that perfunctory law whereby the ages free themselves from the muffling oblivion of mankind; that poking, freakish finger that heredity sticks in our eyes, as we peer anxiously to see if the veil be decorously thrown over all. The tears it brings—that mocking inexorable finger!—are not always of those which purify our mental vision; and of the Silverdales' sight, so far as that concerned itself with this slender, humorous maiden, it had made miniature havoc.

That, after all these dear mediocre centuries, he should re-assert himself—that ancestor, who in the days of Herrick and Suckling had held his own wittily, gloriously, with the best of them! One might have hoped that decades upon decades of ignoring, of snubbing, would have quelled his ghostly essence, would have taught his undying part that at any rate it was not wanted among the posterity of his race. But (and the situation really had its pathetic side) here it was, with the *flair* of these uncanny insubstantialities, finding a welcome at last (though not perhaps of the most rapturous) in the great—great—oh, *je vous le donne en mille!*—in the thousandth great-niece, Lucille Silverdale, daughter and sister of, in abstract phrase, the Healthy Commonplace of the British Nation. It was rare enough, as I said—that shrinking from, that deprecation of, their sole title to distinction; one longed to trace it back to its source, to discover from what veil *that* impish finger had darted, whether, to add a quaintness the more, he, the wit, the sweet singer of that honeyed age, had been as unwelcome to his family circle as she, the somewhat unwilling inheritress of his genius, was to hers. But of that bygone blazon upon the Silverdale 'scutcheon, it would have been ill-advised, perilous to speak; to Lucille even the subject was painful, and in the most impracticable sort of way.

---

5. *Je vous le donne en mille* is a French expression that roughly translates as "you'll never guess" or "fancy that". Yet the narrator does not seem to use it entirely correctly, as the subsequent reference to thousand suggests.

She did say to me once, in a moment of acute dejection, that in any other family she would probably have been the idol, insufferably thrust for worship upon every new-comer. "But as it is," she finished sadly, though with her unquenchable twinkle, "I am the skeleton, rattling my impossible bones, not in a nice musty hiding-place of my own, but in the comfortable, general family-cupboard, which they can't open without seeing me. And they have to open it every day —before visitors, too!"

If I laughed somewhat oppressively at her analogy, I daresay she divined part of the reason, and didn't wonder that her amazing comicality should have filled my eyes with tears.

Well, skeleton or idol, she was sufficiently lonely. They were all so rudely healthy-minded, so full of the working-out of their rosy-cheeked conception of the *joie de vivre* (if it set one marvelling, and shuddering, that was one's own concern), so insistent in exuberance and jollity, that it was no marvel if they had little time, or inclination to make it, for a dreamer of dreams, a seer of visions, a hearer of the music of the spheres. Not that any of those would have been their definition of Lucille; to them, she was a sentimentalist, a "mooney." Yet, apart from the unnaturalnesses into which she would pathetically force herself, she had her soft appealing wildnesses, her gay roguish outbreaks, her bright apologetic materialnesses.

Seeing it written there—*apologetic*—it comes to me with a flash of annoyed divination that Lucille was an incarnate apology.... I knew we should arrive at something, you and I; and I am proved right before I have really posed you my enigma. We are coming to it now: Why could she not have had the courage of her genius? I'm sure we see it often enough—oftener than enough, perhaps—the cocksure type of young man or woman, who has the courage of his or her talent. The courage! The brazenness, more aptly; don't we know them? and they are clever—oh, clever! Then why wouldn't she be something like them, instead of being one desperate, appealing clutch at the Commonplace? She would do violence to her most delicate feelings, and look absolutely complacent over it. Sometimes it made me swear, sometimes—for it had its humorous side, of course—it merely amused me.

Haven't I heard her twanging a banjo, and singing, in that ethereal voice of hers, the last banalities? Haven't I seen her playing at hockey? Seen her! the smile she wore, the nervous conciliatory smile; the runs she took—of all futilities! the hits she made—or didn't make! Lucille's hockey was a triumph of failure. And she *would* say she liked it, afterwards: it was hard, then, to repress one's ironic impulse; one felt that she deserved something. But it wasn't at all that I found it a degradation, or even a derogation, for her to play hockey—that wasn't in the least my feeling. It was more an irritated kind of pity for her fatuity, her lack of humour.

Yet with humour she was otherwise fully equipped; her eyes caught your flying sparkle, and rayed it off into immensity of fun. Her lips—they almost sparkled, too, so mobile, scarlet. Her very hands dimpled sometimes with laughter of rosy finger-tips, and suggestion. In a mad moment you might have imagined that her feet, in their small jewelled slippers, were twinkling also, enjoying the joke like the rest!

And, after a scintillation like that, the girl would do or say something so irritating, so painfully, insistently, commonplace. It was incomprehensible, that attitude of hers; she was, as I have told you, my Sphinx of every-day life.

An instance? Oh, as to that, I could overwhelm you with instances. Well, to take the first that occurs—and indeed it is typical enough, I suppose, for my purpose.

I met them down the river one afternoon of last summer—all of them, Mrs. Silverdale, Mamie, Bella, Lucille, and I think, one or two vague, familiar young men. Already I had divined that one of these last (I could barely distinguish one from the other) admired Lucille, and plumed himself hugely upon his good taste, which, to him, indeed, one could imagine, reflected itself almost as bad taste: the sort of bad taste that one implies in "caviare to the general"[6]—with a perfect understanding of the difficulties of caviare.

This mental attitude of Lucille's admirer (I think his name was Willie Ruthven) produced in his demeanour a mingling of patronage, awe, and flippancy that formed an amazing whole. If it sometimes made me long to kick him, that was perhaps an excess of my feeling of championship for the lovely duckling in this complacently plain family; or perhaps it was that her gentle graciousness towards him seemed to me part of that irritating *Apologia* of hers....

To-day, for example, she was sitting apart from the rest, learning, with his assistance, a banjo-atrocity of the newest, and assuming for histrionic completeness a parody of the vilest parody on speech:

> "What I loiked about that party wos,
> They wos all of 'em so refoined,"

She was chanting in that silvery thread of hers, while he held the music-sheet before her. And that was Lucille Silverdale! the "L.S." of *A Trial of Flight*, that exquisite little sheaf of poems which, like fairy-arrows, had stirred the wings of many a shy emotion in our critical hearts—we of *The Appreciator*, most modern of modernities, most *connaissant* of connoisseurs! It was—well, it was ridiculous, of course, but wasn't it painful, too, to see a genius so belittle the gift of the most high gods? Wasn't it almost wicked, blasphemous?

They were encamped in a mist of greenness, their boat fastened to the long bough of a willow that pushed into the water; 'twas an ideal nook for happy lovers, and I wondered hotly if it realised its present indignity, as, eagerly invited by the rest, I drew in my canoe to their hiding-place. I hardly looked at Lucille and her Companion of the Banjo, nor did she say anything by way of

---

6. See *Hamlet* Act II, Scene ii; quality unappreciated by the ignorant.

welcome; she was, I gathered, too deeply absorbed in her musical studies. I hardly looked at her—but I saw her, more clearly than I saw any of the others: a slender, hazel-eyed incarnation of fragrant coolness, lying there, in white and yellow, among her gleaming blue-green cushions, while the sunbeams glinted off every part of the silver and polished wood of her banjo, and her pretty fingers, too, caught the rays on their rings and their rosy opalescent nail-tips. I could have shaken her where she lay: was she enjoying herself, did she like it?

"Now, Miss Silverdale, you forgot your accent there!" corrected Willie Ruthven, in tones that subdued themselves to a growling tenderness—more could not be demanded of his gruff organ—and even while I inwardly blustered, I felt the humour of the moment steal over me irresistibly. *Modern love-making!* Should I do it for *The Appreciator?* Love-making over that blatant ditty to the poet of *A Trial of Flight!*

But Mamie was claiming my attention.

"Mr. Transfield, are you good at riddles? We have a book of them here; come and help us to guess them; they are such fun!"

Riddles—and a book of them! Well, I went and listened to these riddles. Of my help in guessing them, one can say little, nor, indeed, was much opportunity for distinction afforded. Like most posers of enigmas, Mamie had but one ambition—to give you the answer.

"And your sister, does she like riddles too?"

I asked it almost involuntarily, annoyed at their persistent ignoring of her (I don't know whether it was chivalry or—some other feeling, that incensed me so with her exclusion, her isolation); and then, besides, a riddle—even of this kind—must remind me, must so inevitably suggest her to me! I have not guessed that answer, either, and there was no Mamie to tell it me. Perhaps there isn't any? *Dieu sait!*

---

7. *Dieu sait* means "God knows".

"Lucille—oh, *Lucille*! She never guesses anything, never even tries or listens; too much absorbed by intellectual pursuits!"

"For instance?" I queried, eyebrows irresistibly elevated in my glance at the couple in the bow. I caught her look for an instant—it seemed to say something, hope something ... then, her fingers swept over the strings, and once more she studied the Cockney dialect....

"Anything is better than talking to the rest of us," said Mrs. Silverdale, crossly; to such good purpose was the girl's martyrdom! for martyrdom, I was sure of it, her eyes had but now implied. My heart swelled, my cheek burned, as usual.

Of the rest of the day it needs not to tell you; an epitome of it is there, in the banjo, the cushions, Willie Ruthven, the riddles, and the increasing crossness of the others. For, to add a hopelessness the further, one could more than guess that Mamie desired Willie for herself. Bella, more fortunate, chattered intermittently with the other familiar vagueness; and in our ears the strings incessantly tinkled, the Cockney dialect futilely twanged, Willie's growling tendernesses reverberated....

To Lucille I never once spoke.

But alone, all the way home, through the dusky gleaming of the water, I seemed to catch again that shy elusive glance, that appealing proud humility—that half-divined, wholly-lost answer.

Well, that is all! I wonder if I thought right? I wonder if, by these halting half-apprehensions of mine, these unilluminative side-lights, this one meaningless—or significant?—instance, I have succeeded in gaining at least your interest, your sympathy, for my Sphinx of South Kensington? I wonder if I have helped you to an idea of her, at all corresponding to what she is? And, more than all, I wonder can you divine (for I cannot) where it is that her weakness lies, what it is that makes her so spoil, so desecrate herself?

To me she is the riddle—shall I say, of my life? I almost think that, without exaggeration, I may call her so, for it is more than unlikely now that I shall ever know the answer. Oh, of course, you may say that she has answered it herself, and in the roughest black-and-white, the worst, the bluntest, of type—for you saw, no doubt, as I did, that announcement in the morning's paper, that hateful, incredible juxtaposition of names: "Ruthven-Silverdale." ...

But, you see, I *can't* get that look out of my thoughts, that flutter of the wings of her strange, sweet, mistaken soul—and I think, I can't help thinking, that Lucille has written out her *Apologia* to the last word.

And, in the name of Reason, what was the meaning of it all? Oh, it sets my heart aching, but it makes me angry too; it seems as if—as if—it seems (confound it!) as if I had had something given to me to do—and hadn't done it.

What do *you* think? I hardly hoped you would understand, you know—but perhaps you do. Oh, it is a presumptuous notion, even Willie Ruthven's triumph can't make me think it anything but a presumptuous notion—but a preposterous one? You would scarcely call it that, I think? Would you?

I suppose it is useless to expect you to answer.

Photographs (*Things That No One Tells*, 1910)

"And these people who have come lately—the Baileys: they're great friends of yours, are they not?" one of a group of callers at Runnimede inquired of Lucy Malet.

"Great friends?" she hesitated. "Well, you know we've moved about so much! For years we hadn't seen them."

"But they say they've known you all their lives," the visitor protested. "Isn't it so?"

"Oh yes," she answered, "I suppose, in a sense, we've known them all our lives. But great friends? Is it quite the same thing?"

When it was said, she felt a little ashamed of herself, and the callers emphasized the feeling for her by exclaiming in praise of one of the newcomers.

"Such a sweet girl!"

The chorus instantly followed.

"Yes—so sweet."

"So good-natured."

"Oh, good-natured!" Sylvia Malet agreed. But the perversity which lay in both the girls drove her to Lucy's pitfall, made her add, "A little too good-natured. Do you like good-nature? Don't you find it often a little superfluous, what you had rather have been without?" And then she, in her turn, felt annoyed with herself. Why could she not have simply assented?

In her turn too she was to endure the visitors' fervent contradiction; so that at last she and Lucy were left with a confused perception of themselves as sharp-tongued, cynical, conceited.

"And really we are *not*," they ruefully consoled one another. "Only, the Baileys! ... Well, come and call there to-morrow; we must."

In fact, it was a visit which could not be avoided. Lucy had said, "We've known them all our lives." It was true, yet it was not true. In the wandering life that had been the Malets'—a life nomadic within the straitest limits, but still nomadic—they had gone from one place to another, spending many or fewer years in each; and inevitably even so small a portion of the gipsy's lot had given them something of the gipsy's outlook—its qualities and defects of perception and feeling. Just a little wilder, gayer, freer, but also just a little harder, a little more detached from neighbourliness and "good-nature," were Lucy and Sylvia Malet than the companions of each new home. The mark of the nomad was upon them; the feeling, "We don't *belong* to the place!" was implicit in everything they thought, in almost everything they did, regarding it.

And now at last, by a caprice of officialdom, they had been sent back to a neighbourhood which, long and long ago, they had inhabited—when Lucy had been a wide-eyed "tiny," and Sylvia a baby of the women's kisses. In the years, how countless had been the changes! Looking back occasionally, with the help of their parents' reminiscences, the girls would seem to see almost a revolution, social, economic, intellectual—the keen view of the bird, as it were, upon the places and the people from which they had successively winged their flights.

"And the Baileys haven't stirred till now!"

"I rather wish they hadn't *now!*" said Lucy. "When we met May Bailey last year at those Races ... well, we didn't fall in love exactly, did we?" "Such a sweet girl—so good-natured!" was Sylvia's rejoinder.

Lucy took it unexpectedly. "I believe we *ought* to like her—I really do, Via. We've got some crooked turn in us; we have no hearts or something. I don't know what's the matter with us. Let us make up our minds to think them nice! After all, every woman has some likeness with every other. We'll make straight for the essentials." She laughed. "I won't have him calling me a Superior Person!" Her merry, yet half-wistful gaze was on a photograph, in a plain silver frame, which stood on her toilet-table. "Are you going to stop calling me that?" she asked it fictively. "Are you going to believe that I have a heart of my very own?"

"He knows *that*, if he known nothing else about you, my dear!" Sylvia laughed.

"How dare you know it?" Lucy once more attacked her silent victim.

"But you know it too—about him, I mean."

Lucy faced round. "No! That's just what I don't."

"Why not?"

"I can't *feel* it," she answered slowly. She held the picture closer. "A photograph always makes me shy! Don't stare at me so unflinchingly, my friend.... No, Via; he doesn't look as if he ... *I* don't know! Does he?"

"As if he—what?" was mercilessly required of her?

"'Liked' me, then! ... Let me see if your true love does. Where is he?" she laughed.

"Isn't he there?" said Sylvia, in a incredibly careless voice.

"Oh, I remember now. I was trimming a hat and he took up too much room, so I bundled him into a drawer." She produced the photograph.

Lucy took it. "I think he *does* 'look as if he did.' ... A sort of fervour—"

"Oh, that's becoming to his eyes." Again the tone was unnatural. Lucy turned. "Why, Via, *you* surely haven't any misgivings!"

"Who hasn't?" Sylvia murmured, her soft cheek coloured lightly.

The other sighed. "I didn't know.... What does it all mean—all this figurative walking in the dark?"

"It's better than the light, I dare say," Sylvia cried; and both, losing their serious vein as unaccountably as they had found it, laughed at the little irony. This was how it often was with them. They could be beguiled of their dark moods by an epigram or a paradox, would talk out the trouble, spare themselves in no wise—enjoying the exercise of their wit, yet half-wishing, nevertheless, that they did not see quite so clearly, that they *could* be "taken in"!

For each was at the hour dissatisfied; and on the morrow, as they went to make their call, there was a return of the gloomier outlook—inspired perhaps by the long country road that stretched before them in the coming winter's dreariness.

"Peace at any price," was Sylvia's cry.

"Life at any price," retorted Lucy; but then with a shrug, "*This* isn't life!"

"No, it's death," mourned Sylvia. "At any rate, it's deadly."

"Courage, my dear, courage!" Lucy said. "Here we are! Put on our pretty little masks—oh, it's all enchanting, it's all delightful. We haven't a wish in the world, we haven't a regret: golden fruits tumble into our laps all day, we don't know what to do with 'em all—is Mrs. Bailey at home?"

Mrs. Bailey was at home. The Malets entered. In the hall, a group of departing visitors met them, escorted by some daughters of the house.

"Why, it's the Malets!" a shrill voice cried.

"Yes, May—glad we've found you at home."

"Mother, it's Lucy and Sylvia Malet. I've often told mother what horrid girls you were!" May said, between the kisses—for kissing was the fervently followed order of the day.

"Here's Carrie, Sylvia! Lucy, here's Mabel. This is Gertie, Sylvia!"—and at the end a giggle: "Don't get mixed! This is *Bob*; but he'd be very glad of the chance, you know."

The kindness and the welcome overflowed. In the drawing-room, it was a medley of voices and faces, pulsing, beaming with cordiality. Mrs. Bailey examined the visitors with tearful, smiling eyes—'twas the hour for reminiscences, for recallings of childhood's days. To Lucy and her sister, that brought its annoyance.

"Do you remember, Lucy, how you and Bob used to be sweethearts?"—and then to look at Bob! "Sylvia, you don't remember—but I do—how you used to spit in my face. You *were* a naughty baby! ..."

And through all the irritation and dissembling, the visitors felt ashamed to think of their hesitations, their sense of difference even now. Such kindness as it was—wholehearted, unrestrained!

"We're mean little snobs—we're paltry little wretches. Have *we* got in our whole composition a trace of this warm-heartedness?" Thus they raged at themselves, and all the while they laughed and talked, infected by the glow of the reunion, until at last, tea over, the Bailey girls proposed a visit to their own domain.

"Our glory-hole, where we take our *special* friends."

("It's only a cold-hearted little toad like myself," Lucy Malet inwardly exclaimed, "that could wonder who are their acquaintances, if we are special friends.")

"Yes," cried Carrie, the family wit. "And our 'special smoke,' too. Ah, Sylvia's shocked at that. It's only to keep the boys company."

"The boys, yes—the *boys*," May underlined it with a wink at Lucy. "Lucy's shocked, too, Carrie! We only take a 'cig' now and then on the sly, you know, Lucy." Then very seriously, "Of course, we don't *really* smoke; it's so unlady-like. Don't you think so?"

"Oh, atrocious," Lucy burlesqued it; "the last stage of depravity—to smoke really. Only, how do you smoke *un*really?"

"Just get 'him' to light it for you, you know. That's the important part," Mabel informed her; then in her turn she added, with an almost religious solemnity, "But of course we wouldn't *really* smoke, you know."

The ethics of cigarette-smoking had been the staircase topic; they had attained the glory-hole, and now—the Malets felt it in the air; the Baileys had thought of little else from the beginning—*now* the genuine business of the afternoon was to be put in hand.

By chance, the Malets had both taken the same side of the long table that almost filled the room, while on the other side was ranged the row of Baileys—moving, ever moving from chimneypiece to cupboard, from bracket to table-drawer, until at last the fire began—for it had all the air of a bombardment. There were skirmishes. "Nonsense, Gertie, that's mine." "Yours, indeed! he gave it to *me*." "Well, never mind now; show it." "Where's that one of Billy?" "*You* ought to know. Under your pillow perhaps...."

Photograph upon photograph shot across the table—all of men.

The visitors picked up card after card, examined, shivered, perplexedly gave opinions; but their judgments had to vary—politeness, good-feeling, and other more stringent rules in the game demanded it, so when a feature was susceptible of any word of praise, that feature became the prominent one. "Nice eyes." "A good nose." They were then at liberty to say something of what they really thought about some other picture.

"I don't like this face," Sylvia thus declared.

It was taken quite good-humouredly. "Ah, but he's a good sort. Will do anything in the world for you—"

"Except marry you," another girl complained.

"And who wants to marry him, may I ask?" the first voice shrilled.

"No one, I should hope," Lucy Malet dryly said, inspecting the photograph. If for her it spelt out every letter of distaste, repulsion, she still could see that the claim of "awfully good-looking" which had heralded its career across the table might by some be taken seriously. The straight-lined blatant image, vacuous beyond belief, with monocled eye and fur-collared coat—oh, what meant vulgarity, if this meant aught else? and yet, there *were* the regular features and the thickly waving hair, plume-like on the showy forehead....

"Ha-ha! you're taking a second look, Lucy."

"Don't cut me out, mind. He's in town every Saturday, regularly. He's the principal solicitor in Ballyvourney."[8]

"Yes, and very well off. A good spec, Lucy."

"You think I might succeed in getting him to do the one thing he won't do—marry me?" Lucy said ironically.

"Ah, I'm afraid not. He'd flirt with you to the top of his bent, like he does with every one—"

"Would he?" She could not keep the edge off her voice. "I wonder if he has the remotest idea what 'flirting' means?"

"*Hasn't* he then?" three voices almost reverently assured her.

Something was stronger than she! "Are you sure *you* have?"—and then she felt alarmed: that was a little too sharp?

But such a question could seem to the Baileys only the sheerest chaff. "Oh, not the slightest!" they radiantly retorted.

"Well, we've looked at that long enough—unless Lucy would like to linger longer? 'Ling longer, Loo'."

But others were produced. "Now, this is Carrie's only love."

"What do you think of *this?* Don't look at Gertie!" "Ah, he's the real one; but he's such a rascal"—and mournfully was regarded a round-eyed rustic, invested with such suggestions of manliness and conquest as leggings and a whip can furnish. "And he's a nephew of Lady Simpson's—so *he's* good enough for you, at any rate. Only he's such a villain—you never can tell whether he means it or not."

At last all were shown: on the table, beneath the blinding lamp, the hoarded collection lay. Photographs within frames, without

---

8. Ballyvourney is a village in southwest County Cork in Ireland.

frames, large photographs, small photographs, "midgets," "postage-stamps," the gamut of the photograph—old, middle-aged, new; pale brown, dark brown, platino-type; glazed, unglazed, in one or two disastrous instances coloured.... The various owners could not conceal their pride. Had ever a mere quartette of girls so glorious, so monstrous, a collection?

"Have you and Sylvia as many as that?" Carrie glowing cried.

"No, indeed we haven't," Sylvia assured her.

"You must show us, mind. It'll be our turn next."

"I haven't any," they both protested, but it was scoffed at.

"Oh, nonsense. Why, you can always have a photograph for the asking."

"What about 'the asking,' thought?" Sylvia said.

"Oh, they don't mind. They like it.... Have them all ready for us to give our verdicts."

"*I* know something, too!" May Bailey tittered. "Something about a lovely silver frame, on Lucy's toilet-table. I've heard about that frame. Ours are nothing to it."

The strewage on the table answered that with bold defiance. Lucy surveyed the riot of colour, form, and medium. "But yours are gorgeous," she murmured.

"They *are* nice. But yours—real silver! It's very plain, though, isn't it?" (May consoled herself.) "But the lot it must have cost!"

"You see I had only one to get.... But how did you hear about it?" she reluctantly inquired.

"A little bird—!"

"Servants tell tales," said Mabel archly.

"So you'll have to show us yours, Lucy, remember. And Sylvia, too—but *she's* deep, she keeps hers hidden. Who is he, Lucy?"

"The Man in the Iron Mask," Lucy solemnly told her.

"We'll find out, never fear. Trust *us!*"

"But we must go," said Lucy. The long string of good-byes began, the kisses and the messages—but at last they escaped, while gay shrill calls pursued them.

"Don't forget!"

"Remember, Lucy—you're to show us the Man in the Iron Mask. How *inconvenient* it must be.... But never mind; you've got his photo, just like us."

They looked at one another in the starlight, between merriment and misery.

"Yes—yes! Oh, Via, we *have* a crooked turn in us, we have no hearts or something.... Wasn't it terrible? ... They were so kind, and we said we'd make for the essentials. Well," she hid her face in her muff—"I've got 'his photo,' just like them."

The Boulevardiers (*Things That No One Tells*, 1910)

Colonel Roche and his three pretty daughters had found that they could give, out of their holiday, only a shredded week to Paris, and already four days had gone by—it was the fifth, the penultimate; yet nothing had happened which even the schoolgirl Carrie could reckon among occurrences. The days had been for the girls (and they suspected, for their father) merely a blank, dull whirl of churches, galleries, English restaurants; the boulevards in a cab, the Bois in a cab, everything in a cab. For the Colonel, recklessly cautious, drove everywhere; it was ruinous, but his mistrust prevailed—his mistrust of the pavement, of the atmosphere, of above all, his convoy.

"These Frenchmen!" and "Those girls!" The phrases were recurrent, and they summed up his attitude. He looked forward in secret to a later, solitary visit, and could resign himself for the moment to the institution of a despotism tempered by sight-seeing. So the little party plunged into Cimmerian churches,[9] tramped through glittering museums and glowing galleries, drove back to solid "English" meals—until at last it had come to be true,

---

9. Cimmerian literally means "related to the ancient tribe of the Cimmerii", but is used proverbially "as a qualification of dense darkness, gloom, or night, or of things or persons shrouded in thick darkness" (*OED Online*).

even to be unconcealable, that the girls were flatly disappointed. *This* the Gay City! Was the title, then, ironical?

Every morning the trio had their silent, telegraphed hope: to-day they would join perhaps the enchanted army of the strollers, idlers, gazers—glancers!

The glancers. It was with these that they were most conscious of affinity; for already, despite difficulties, they had been cheered by delicious tiny triumphs. Delightfully, dark eyes had looked; flatteringly, dark heads had been twisted, dark moustaches called into play.... And then the girls had been jolted out of sight! They realised, however, that if they could thus carry the situation from the depths of a cab (as to which the Colonel's choice was invariably of the dingiest) they might, with the wider opportunities of an evening's wandering, achieve little masterpieces in the intercourse of the eyes.

Every morning, then, brought its hopes, and every morning the same desolating programme frustrated them. The hotel would have been left behind by but a yard or two when the detested signal would be given; the—almost they called it—"hearse" would lumber alongside to jerk their hopes and visions to the daily funeral. Nita, prettiest of the pretty three, radiant in fresh cambric, would first be interred—soft frills and sparkling shoes irretrievably wasted; then would come Kathleen, conscious of the slimmest, roundest, most engaging little figure, that now no one could do more than guess at; last of the three followed Carrie, newly from school, tiny, yet so cleverly complete that her very delicacy and finish were the reasons for her reduction, in the cab, to insignificance. Only her eyes—of a blue, of a grey, of a depth!—only her eyes rescued Carrie.

When the Colonel had flustered and stumbled to his place, amid growls and comparisons injurious, they would roll gloomily off—to another church, another gallery or museum.

"And they're beautiful, you know," the girls assured one another; "they're wonderful! Only—"

"They're not what we want," Carrie, in her crudity, came out with.

"Oh, as to *wanting*," Nita repressed her, "it isn't so much that one wants anything different—" She stopped, recoiling from self-analysis.

"Just to look into the shops, and—*that*," Kathleen supplied. "What we do is too improving, too "educational." But of course that is what we were brought here for," she sighed. "To be finished."

"Well, if you and Nita were brought here to be finished, what was *I* brought for?" Carrie demanded, sore under her snubbing.

"To be begun, child," Nita loftily said.

The schoolgirl looked at her inimitably. "I begin where you leave off, then!" she cried. "I wonder where I'll end." She performed an admirably foreign little shrug. "I've got it, I've got it! Look—just like Papa's favourite waiter, isn't it? After all, there's *some* fun to be got out of Paris." She watched appealingly for applause and acquiescence. But the others were finding the pricks too sharp.

"Don't mimic waiters, Carrie," Kathleen reproved her. "I dare say a child like you can get amusement out of that sort of thing. Of course, I like Paris; it's"—she sought a word, only to fall back again upon the condemnatory—"wonderful! But one feels somehow that one hasn't entered into the real *life* of the place when one drives everywhere, and goes to the English places for everything. Doesn't one, Nita?"

"We might as well be in Dublin," Nita bitterly responded.

Carrie felt a wave of sympathy. It *was* a shame: here was Nita, saying in Paris that they might as well be in Dublin! Generous, forgetful of injuries, the little sister hastened to bring solace.

"Ah no, Nita!" She said, in her insinuating brogue. "Don't say that, now. It's more fun than *that*, bad as it is. And I wonder you don't think so; for it's you that gets the most of it. The way they look at you, I mean." Her eyes sparkled.

The others stared. "Carrie! The way they look at you—" But

it was useless; smiles rippled irrecoverably at the phrase, the reminiscence. Well, since Carrie—little wretch—had torn away the veil! ... The pretty creatures drew together, smiling, glancing, chattering.

And (was it the reward for their virtue of frankness?) at last, that evening, the Colonel relented.

Dinner had been a success. He had achieved his favourite corner, his favourite shrugging waiter, and the fare had been delectably British—solid, sanguine, straightforward. In the afternoon, too, he had for the first time attempted French conversation with a handsome counter-lady in a cigar-shop, and it had been wellnigh a triumph. She had smiled and sparkled, had even retorted. What she had retorted, indeed, he had not perfectly comprehended; but that had passed unnoticed—a look had answered, "*un regard de militaire*." [10] *Dame*! one understood this part of the business, since all the world over 'twas the same!

"What do you say, girls, to a stroll this evening?" had been the delightful upshot of it all. "A lounge on the boulevard—and back by the Place de l'Opéra, eh?"

It had almost taken away their breath, but they had had the cunning to display only a tepid pleasure. Nita had consulted Kathleen, and Kathleen Carrie; they had each in turn hung fire a little.

"Oh, if you don't care about it, you can stay behind. A funny lot of girls you are! Any others would jump at the idea of an evening's walk in the best-lighted city in the world. One thing I can tell you: if you aren't content to walk, you must stay at home for the rest of the time. I can't afford this incessant driving. It was all very well before I knew my way about; but for to-night and to-morrow, you may as well make up your minds for a little more exercise.... Do you intend to come—any of you—or not?"

"Oh yes, Papa," Nita the spokeswoman said. "Of course we are

---

10. *Un regard de militaire* means "the look (or air) of a military man".

coming; and I am sure it will be very nice. Shall we go and get ready now?"

"Don't take an hour about it," he grimly warned them. They disappeared. On the stairs they exchanged only glances; but their room once gained, it was who should skip highest, hug tightest. And then, with the excitement, Carrie had an inspiration.

"If we were to give Papa the slip ...?" she whispered, bright-eyed, unprincipled. "Kathleen, Nita—are you game?"

Kathleen nodded. It was Nita, then, who hesitated? And Nita—such ever was life's way!—openly the Colonel's favourite, was the only one of them all who had pocket-money, the only one who could take them anywhere. *She* visibly flinched, *she* hadn't the pluck: is it not always the penniless who are readiest to lead forlorn hopes?

A little crossly in the end, the three descended—charming in their fresh attire—and found the Colonel in the vestibule, ostentatiously awaiting them. They started, Nita in front, with the father, Kathleen and Carrie following; but during their passage of the Rue St. Lazare there was nothing conspicuously more brilliant than usual to rejoice them. Hope lived, however; and as they turned into the Rue de Rome, where the glittering boulevard filled in the horizon, their eyes brightened correspondingly, their lips broke into gayer curves, their feet felt ready for dancing. Carriages rolled by on their way to the Opera; within them, ravishing toilets were subtly suggested by the beauty of the mere concealing cloaks.... The girls again grew restless, reckless: why couldn't they, too, go to the Opera? Was it imaginable that the Colonel, if they should propose it, would consent?

"He never would," Kathleen sighed.

"But we might try!" vehement Carrie whispered; and, as though she had been overheard by the couple in front, on the instant their steps slackened (she felt a horrid little revulsion of sheer nervousness) ... they stopped ... they came back.

"You girls wait outside," commanded the Colonel, "while I

go in here and get some cigarettes. Be careful; behave yourselves; remember that you aren't in Dublin."

He disappeared. It cannot be denied that when he *was* reckless, he was quite inconceivably so.

"It's the same shop he was in this afternoon," clever Carrie told them; "where he talked French, you remember. Considering that then he bought quite a big box of cigarettes ...!" They giggled, a little scornful, yet a little envious too. He could, it seemed, get his "fun," even in Paris. And at his age! Here were they, young, pretty (they knew it), and they had not had a morsel.... Oh, it was a shame. The secular feminine anger surged in their hearts. At *his* age!

In the end: "Let us give him the slip!" Carrie once more urged them. "Doesn't he deserve a good fright? Just look! She's getting down boxes and boxes; it'll never be over."

"Even driving is better than this," Kathleen almost whimpered. They gazed tumultuously, dimly, at their glimpse of the boulevard, with its lights, its strollers, its immeasurable, innumerable assurances of the joy of life. And they were here—pent, humbly waiting, in this horrid little street.

"Are you going to stop here for him all night?" Carrie reiterated her war-cry. "Oh, Kathleen, if Nita's afraid, come *you!*"

But Nita's silence was that of the hero before the deed. "Look here!" she whispered. "It really is too bad for Papa. We'll pay him out, properly. I've got money.... Let us come, and—and go somewhere."

Her companions, in their turn, hesitated. Wide-eyed, the three envisaged one another. At last they faltered away from the cigar-shop window. Courage grew with movement: they walked decisively on. But in a last supreme vacillation they looked back. Still they could discern the counter-lady—gracious, voluble—empilling her bright packages, while the Colonel, debonair and conquering, examined, pronounced, compared.

"He'll be there for the next half-hour!"

They trotted, gaily chattering, down the little Rue de Rome. Almost they had decided to visit the Opera; Nita had enough to pay for tolerable places. The Opera—yes! At the entrance from the street to the boulevard, they came to an enchanted pause, taking the impression before their plunge into the movement and glitter. Ah, this was it at last; this *was* Paris. The gay idleness, the busy gaiety, the strollers, gazers ... glancers. Now one would see what one could do!

They stood there, free. And, "If any one should speak to us!" breathed Nita.

"We shall know what to do," dauntless Carrie asserted. "Come on."

"... Yes," and "In a second," said both her elders at once. "In a second, child...."

"I wonder how Papa is getting on," Nita giggled. "He isn't coming, I hope?"

Kathleen peered over her shoulder. "No.... Oh no, thank goodness," she added, with an amazing little titter.

Carrie was grimly examining them. "Are we coming on?"

"Wait till we settle what places to ask for."

"We know the price of the only places we can go to."

Nita burnt a boat. "Will you ask, then?"

The schoolgirl stared, did flinch a little, but, "Oh, if you're afraid," she declared, though with a flutter at the heart, "I don't mind. They won't eat us.... Well?"

"Shall we not try the Opera at all?" Kathleen came to the rescue of her elder: Carrie was so pert, always ready to put herself forward! "It might be hard to manage—"

"I don't see why," grumbled the tactless child.

"A stroll instead, Carrie?" Nita said deferentially. "What do you think?"

"Very well," Kathleen agreed; and with "All right," Carrie grudgingly yielded.

But still they waited. The crowd wandered, individual attention caught frequently by the three, so deliciously rosy and dark-eyed in their attack of the nerves. They were out of the cab, it was the moment for masterpieces; and men were looking, looking again. Two of them, bright-faced, mischievous, bent with confident merriment a little toward the girls' corner—black eyes sparkling, dark pale faces lit with admiration....

Laughing aloud in frank amusement, the two boys passed along the crossing of the Rue de Rome on their way down the boulevard. With shrugs and glances, "*Ce sont des lapines, hein?*" "*Des Anglaises, quoi? On n'est pas plus jolie, mais——*" "*Mais joliment bêtes, mon cher. Regardez-moi donc, comme ça se sauve! On dirait des voleuses.*" He raised a little his light, mocking voice. "*L'on ne suit pas, mes belles, croyez-moi. Ce n'est pas la peine.*"[11]

Their laughter broke irrevocably forth again at the sight of the small scampering figures....

The Colonel, issuing with his neat parcel five minutes later, was apologetic to the gloomy group.

"These Frenchwomen are so talkative! Well, girls, I didn't keep you so long as all that—you needn't treat me to sulks. A quarter of an hour!" He referred to his watch. It had been a generous quarter of an hour. He saw it; but, "Come, don't be sulky," he said again sharply.

Immutably they kept silence, persistently they gazed away from him, away from each other.

"A very foolish display of temper," he observed. "We'd better take a cab, after all, for the rest of the evening." He signalled; their doom drove alongside.

With no exchange of glances, no care for flounces or ribbons, but stolidly, solemnly, with an indescribable effect of limpness, the girls interred themselves; and in now unbroken taciturnity they were jolted by the Place de l'Opéra, the Madeleine, the

---

11. "They're bunnies, eh? Englishwomen? They are pretty enough, but—" "But pretty silly, my friend. Look how they run away. As if they're thieves! [...] Don't worry, sweethearts, we won't follow you. It's not worth it."

Boulevard Malesherbes, back through the Rue de la Pépinière to the hotel.

Desertsurges (*Things That No One Tells*, 1910)

I

Heaton had overtaken Emily Bolton in the avenue, the long, dark avenue that narrowed between its pushing evergreens to the tarnished, ugly house. Desertsurges![12] The name, as he had often commented, was gloomy enough in all conscience, yet it carried a suggestion of romance, of wildness, which made it too high-sounding for the place. That was so flat, so dead, in its sour destitution of all beauty—just a hideous, "unkept-up," Irish country-house.

One, nevertheless, where Heaton for the moment spent many of his days: so that now, on his coming up with the younger Miss Bolton, it was taken by both as the merest matter-of-course that he should be on his way to call there.

"I'm fortunate; my star's in the heaven," he said. "Here you are, coming in precisely at the right moment. Where have you been?"

"At the choir practice," she told him dolorously.

"Ah! that good-looking young curate. Mr. Perry, isn't it?"

She answered with the droll schoolgirl dignity.

"Mr. Perry is the curate; but he's not good-looking. He wasn't there, besides. And I hate the choir practice. I'm perished! I'm longing for the fire and tea. Aren't you?" She hurried along the damp gravel. "How hideous and hateful it is!"

"You mustn't be cross because Mr. Perry deserted the practice. Perhaps he had a cold—curates often have colds, haven't they?"

"I really don't know, Major Heaton. And I don't care whether he's there or not. You know I don't," she murmured precipitately;

---

12. Desertserges is the name of a parish in West Cork with which Mayne may have been familiar, but the name also evokes both the barrenness of life in the country house and Emily's illicit desires.

then caught herself up and laughed nervously. "I'm not cross, but I can't be really nice till we get in"; and coming to the door at last, she pushed it open, they went in—the empty drawing-room confronted them. It was too early as yet for lamps, and the daylight of early October was very bleak and spectral, as through the gaunt window it peered in from a soaked and rusty lawn. The grass there had already the brownness of its winter texture, and the wet brilliance of the fallen leaves upon it added only a sharper note to the effect of dreariness.

Emily Bolton shivered, and buried her chin in the collar of her coat.

"Do you think I might stir the fire?" she asked, advancing a stealthy hand to the poker. "No, I daren't. Aunt Lou would be so angry." Her light blue eyes were comically apprehensive. "It's the sort of fire that you see in a waiting-room. Ugh!"

She looked round the sombre walls, up to the high, yellowed ceiling—then turned suddenly foolhardy. "I *will!* She can't scold me before you."

Heaton, standing near her, preserved his pose of indulgent scrutiny. None knew better than he the spell which a man of middle age can work upon a girl of her years, by the exaggeration of his seniority. A sudden flash of ardour from him! what magical effect it had, contrasted with some former paternal speech, some appeal from age to youth, some air of aloofness, of withdrawnness.... He watched her, smiling in his enigmatic fashion; tall, dark exceedingly, very handsome, and gifted with a manner which was vaguely "foreign" in its suppleness and hinted ardour. The look from his black eyes—the bold, free, conquering, yet questioning look! To think of it could thrill her, to meet it almost frighten her: what did it mean, what did it say? A language new, but growing daily more familiar; a word she did not understand, but which allured, compelled her.

She sprang now, in her sudden courage, to the fender. "There! what a difference a good poking makes"—and truly the room was transfigured in the delicious light. The desolation from outside seemed to peer with something less of ghostliness; the windows, lean and black-framed, lost much of their meagre immensity amid the frisking shadows—and Emily, enchanted, appealed for sympathy. "Isn't it nice? Isn't that better?"

"It's delightful," Heaton said; "but think of Aunt Lou!" He assumed in his turn an awestruck apprehension. "Think of it, if she should scold *me*."

Emily nodded. "She wouldn't dare."

"She dares do all that may become a man," Heaton asseverated.

"And I'm sure no man would dare to scold you."

"I was going on," he answered patiently. "I was going to add, 'who dares do more, is—a woman.'"

"Oh, but that's not the right quotation," she said. "I'm doing *Macbeth* for my reading society. Don't you remember? It is, '*who dares do more, is none*.'"

Heaton passed a hand over his moustache.

"Oh—! I see," she cried. "I've been dull. Like Desertsurges," she petulantly added; "like the place, and the house, and the family."

"Well, it's certainly dull of you not to have some tea and give me some, when there it is," her visitor rejoined. "Toast? I shall finish it, if you are not quick."

The girl stood an instant longer in her dejected attitude, then put off her hat and coat, touched up her hair at the glass, and came at last to the tea-table. Almost absently, she began to fill the cups. "Ah, but isn't it true," she murmured, "isn't it?" Her eyes were clouded.

"That Desertsurges—?"

"Is dull; that the town is duller; that we—the Desert people—are dullest of all, Major Heaton."

The quaver in the childish voice amused him; he laughed, he chose another little square of toast, then told her teasingly, "Oh, dull, dull, dull, Miss Emily. And yet," he added in a lower tone, "I stay here."

"Yes," she said, and blushed helplessly. "The hunting—"

"The hunting." He underlined it, with merciless eyes upon her mounting colour. "That is of course what keeps me."

He had known so well that she would answer that by looking! ... Sometimes it occurred to Heaton with amazement that he should be doing this. Where was the attraction? Emily Bolton was pretty, yes—but of prettiness he had had such endless experience, and experience of so much more interesting a kind. For though she was pretty, she was very little more. So young (eighteen!) but crude, not exquisite, she had none of that pearl-like charm which glimmers from the one girl in a hundred of her age, that touching effect at once of transiency and perfection. No; she had none of that, he thought, as lying back in his arm-chair he scrutinised her. The signs of breeding—mere inheritance!—were there; even in the ill-assured and sometimes flippant manner, one could trace a long tradition of refinement; the voice, the intonation, the turning of a phrase, the score of nothings which unconsciously proclaim us or betray—all these for Emily were friends, not traitors. It was when one passed such boundaries, seeking the individual, that one was disappointed. Heaton had often felt it, even while he searched the face and found indeed no meagreness of form or tint: how soft and round and coloured was the cheek, how well-set were the light blue eyes, how delicate the nose, and curved the upper lip. The hair was gold—theoretically, as with most men, his favourite colour (and yet the woman of Heaton's life had been as dark-locked as himself!); the whole effect was of a prettiness complete and charming, and—again he observed it with satisfaction—a well-bred prettiness into the bargain. Heaton would not, in fact, have known how to think of himself if he had found that even a hint of unbreeding could come from a woman whom, meeting in society, he had singled out. But there *was* something wrong! And, aware of himself as no seeker after the soul, he was puzzled to discover what it might be. For he had accepted her frankly, with her many limitations—never looking for wit, for subtlety, for knowledge; and, not looking for them, surely undeceived by their absence?

What did keep him here, in his little country-hole, where the boasted hunting was not of the first class—what kept him here? What brought him daily to Desertsurges? Not Aunt Lou and not Elizabeth, the elder sister of his little friend: most assuredly not Elizabeth! Well, of course it was Emily: so much he acknowledged—but, good Heavens, why? She positively bored him sometimes. Heaton, lying back in comfort, staring at the fire, told himself with a sudden snap of cynicism that it would be perfect if he were but alone. To be aware of that expectant little countenance, to know that sooner or later you would have to glance around with meaning—meaning what? he never knew exactly—'twas a bore, after all.

For how long had he been silent? He turned his head; his eyes had all the glamour that she watched for avidly.

"*May* I talk?" he asked. "I've really been afraid. Such a brown study! What were you puzzling out?"

"You," she disconcertingly replied.

"Me! I'm as simple as the A B C—which you can hardly have forgotten yet."

"It took me a very long time to learn it," she laughed. "Even now I have to repeat it all over before I'm certain whether W or U comes first."

"Oh—I, of course," he told her gravely.

She wrinkled very faintly indicated eyebrows. ("Perhaps that's it?" he thought precipitately, looking at her the while with all the brilliant boldness; "perhaps that's the want?")

"I should think 'I' always did come first," she ventured, dimpling; but he interrupted her—the opportunity was too facile!

"Yes. So should I think that ... *you* always did come first"; and his rich voice, in its stress upon the pronoun, conveyed everything but an accusation of selfishness.

The girl looked up, with darkened, lustrous eyes; she trembled almost visibly beneath the look.

"Don't laugh at me," she faltered. "Don't! I know I'm very stupid—"

"Ah!" he cried, half rising. "You're *not*. You're cleverer than you know. Emily, little Emmie"—he came towards her vehemently: she waited, helpless and adoring, looking downward now with wide, blind eyes....

The handle of the door twisted sharply, but a towering screen allowed an instant's grace: enough for Heaton. He was propped against the mantelpiece, with only the smouldering of his black eyes to betray his anger, when Elizabeth Bolton made her appearance.

"Emmie! I didn't know you had come in. How-do-you-do, Major Heaton?" She greeted him uncordially; his manner, too, lost something of its suavity for her—he was so furious! and at any time he disliked her, she was his most detested of all types, the tall, pale, grave-eyed country and county maiden. He was certain that she spied upon her pretty sister, that what he called "the inevitable jealousy" expressed itself in looking after her—nothing, he could well imagine, more galling to the little one!

Nevertheless, he hoped now that the little one was not going to be foolish, to show temper, to "give them away." He glanced at her uneasily. She *was* pouting, she *was* tapping a restless foot.... Heaton felt again the profound conviction that it would not do; and yet, was he going to be baffled by this other?

"You've warded off a serious quarrel," he began. "Miss Emily and I were getting angry over the alphabet. Fighting over the A B C." He smiled sardonically for his own amusement, thinking how all too apt his explanation was.

"The railway guide, or the real thing?" Elizabeth asked, accepting her tea from the ungracious little hand that held it towards her at a stretch.

"The real genuine old thing," Heaton rattled on. "Your sister tells me she never succeeded in learning it."

"And you were teaching her?"

He laughed and flashed ostentatiously a look towards Emily. "Yes," he drawled. "I was trying to teach her the difference between U and I."

"They're a long way apart," Elizabeth said. "I should have thought the difference was plain enough." Her eyes met his unflinchingly: it was as though she accepted a challenge.

"One is certainly a great deal in front of the other," he acquiesced. "May I have another cup of tea?"

He went to the table, standing thus between the sisters; and now Emily was under the dominion of the burning look—never (as she realised, half-triumphant, half-alarmed), never so insistent, so resistless, in all the times before.

She handed him the rattling cup and saucer.

"You've forgotten the sugar," he objected.

With a nervous laugh, she indicated the bowl.

"But it's so difficult to help myself," he pleaded.

"You know what these cups are. Yes—two lumps!" and, the little service paid, his victory complete, he once more took his place beside the fire and glanced at his antagonist.

Some years older though she was than Emily, Elizabeth was too young for the baffling of such subtleties as these: the sense of defeat was plain for him to read there. Her usually calm brown eyes were bright with annoyance, her cheek was flushed, her lip bitten—and Heaton was content. He had proved to her that he was master of the situation: now he would consent to make himself agreeable. And for the remainder of his stay he *was* agreeable, was merely the gay, delightful visitor for both—vivid, enigmatic, with the air of middle age incessantly assumed, the pose of sadness charmed away by youth, the hint of mystery, of "life," all the sorcery that such a man has at command; and that, in these surroundings, was almost absurdly facile in effect. He found that part ready, and he played it well, telling himself it bored him—but it did not bore him.

Underneath, however, there now lay the keen resolve to baffle the elder girl. What business had she to circumvent him? what business, if it came to that, to suppose that he needed circumventing? And Heaton was sage enough to know that all his glamour had not genuinely dazzled Elizabeth. "The sort of woman who never *is* taken in," he commented. "The type that goes for 'solid worth'—and gets it, into the bargain. Poor little Emmie!" he sighed, compassionate. By comparison with the abhorred Elizabeth, Emily was growing endeared to him; he was almost ceasing to wonder why, or to prophesy that it would not do.

"What a time she must have of it, between Aunt Lou and the Elizabeth. A pity one can't get her out of the place—but that's impossible...."

Heaton went thoughtfully down the avenue, and thoughtfully out into the lonely, dreary road that stretched for two long Irish miles to the town of Freshford, where he was staying "for the hunting."

The two girls, left behind, were silent for the first few seconds.

"How did the choir practice go, Emmie?" the elder then inquired.

"How does it always go?" the other yawned. "The same howling and shrieking."

"Was Mr. Pretty there?"

"No, he wasn't," Emily answered curtly. "Any more uninteresting questions?"

Elizabeth laughed. "That used to be an interesting one."

"Used it? ... Where were you?"

"I didn't go out."

"How was it that you didn't see us coming in then—Major Heaton and I?"

"I wasn't at the window," Elizabeth answered with a smile.

"Weren't you really? For once!" the other murmured.

Elizabeth looked up. "What do you mean?"

"You're generally there, aren't you?" said the insolent little voice.

"And if I am—?"

"Why, you see things, of course. Isn't that what one goes to windows for?"

"Emily!"

"What have I said?" she demurely asked.

The sister looked at her, in poignant stress of feeling; then took her resolution and said nothing in reply. "Well, he stayed so long that it's time to dress for dinner," she remarked. "Come along! there's no use in putting Aunt Lou into a rage. She has been cross all day." And with a heavy sigh and yawn, Elizabeth added, "She always is, when Uncle Tom's hunting."

"Oh—was there a meet to-day?" cried Emily alertly.

"Yes, but a bad covert. I suppose that is why Major Heaton wasn't out," Elizabeth said.

"Of course," the younger girl assented, hiding a small grimace behind her picked-up hat and coat. "Just fancy, if I had left these in the drawing-room!" she giggled; and, restored to mutual good-humour by the sense of a "row" escaped, the two girls hurried to their dressing.

"If only we could have asked him to stay!" Emily said wistfully. "Other girls can do these things, or have them done for them.... Is Aunt Lou very bad, Bessie?" she added; and "Very" came in answer, with an abysmal sigh.

Emily clasped her hands behind her neck. "How are we to stand it?" she groaned.

The other girl glanced apprehensively. "I suppose there are worse things," she faltered. "And Uncle Tom's a dear!"

"Yes, he's a dear. But how long is one to go on? Suppose it *never* changes?" The child might have been gazing into the very abode of woe, so set was her little face, so tragic in its wanness.

"Everything changes, some time or other," was all the comfort that Elizabeth's philosophy could impart. "Come along; you'd better. That was the second gong."

They went, very timorously, downstairs to dinner.

II

The rain which that day had seemed satisfied, content to go to Spain, was on the contrary but recoiling for a fresh onslaught. Past the heavy gates of Desertsurges, a week later, the country road swept blackly in the darkness, but under the light from the lodge-windows it glittered, luridly streaming—almost a turbid river between the low, discoloured hedgerows. The gateposts, the walls of the lodge, were saturated to blackness, and the chrysanthemums, drenched to death in the tiny cottage-garden, hung, turning brown upon their swaying branches, drearily above the glutinous mosaic of dead leaves that paved the beds and pathways. Heaton, in his recent visits, had often mused upon the knack that Irish people had of letting their "places" look their worst.

Above the rustle and drone of the rain to-night, there grew gradually the nearing, nearer sound of the plunge and splash of horses' feet, and the swishing rumble of wheels. The coachman, Driscoll, lounging sleepily, after an idle day, near the kitchen fire, puzzled lazily over it as it came up to and passed the little gate-house.

"Faith, haven't they done dhrivin' at Charleston yet, then?" he murmured. "And Casey with a cough out of him that'd frighten ye. 'Tisn't often they're so late gettin' home: 'twas that way the carriage was goin'.... Yerra! it isn't them—sure it's stopped quite close. What is it at all then?" Almost wakened by his curiosity, he rose as though to go to the door.

"Will ye stop quiet?" his wife exclaimed; "and not be openin' the door on me and lettin' in a dhraught that'd cut ye in two. Sure, what's the odds, so's they don't want the gate openin'? 'Tisn't far ye'd hear anything to-night, either, with the roads as heavy as your conscience."

The easy-going man laughed at her thrust, and abandoned without reluctance his vague intention of reconnoitering. "As like as not you're right," he answered, and soon was half asleep again before the glowing sods.

The carriage, drawn into a deep bay of the road, waited heavily amid the smoke from the horses' backs, and the denser mist of the close, penetrating rainfall. From time to time, Heaton's head, in a cap that pouched low over the eyes, was thrust forth hastily to peer in the direction of Desertsurges' gloomy gates. It was only half an hour's drive to Freshford,[13] but if there were great delay, they could never catch the mail-train, and if they should lose it—

Was she never coming?

On the avenue, up at the house, the leaves lay as closely pasted as before the gate-lodge; yet Elizabeth, dressing slowly (a good deal too soon for dinner) in her room above the side-entrance, heard suddenly on the terrace something that sounded like their dry, light patter of frosty days. She listened vaguely, her reasoning in abeyance, thinking only how uncanny was their whirling; but at length the accompanying noise of the rain urged itself into her consciousness. How could the leaves drift? for the downfall was undeviating—actually it was crunching the light gravel of the terrace! But no, neither could that be: for this rain was merely a monstrous drizzle, causing no displacement of the tiniest pebble.

All at once, she caught her lip, drew in her breath sharply: rain, rain, and rain, persistent yet fine—it could not sound like that upon the gravel. She went quickly to the window and held back the blind, peering with hands around her eyes into the streaming night; then with a little cry she turned from the outlook, paused for the barest instant—but soon hurried to the wardrobe, tore down a cloak, threw it over her, tugged on her shoes.... "If I can only catch her; I can run twice as fast as she...." Her hands bungled terribly in the frantic hurry, but at last she was ready—fled from the room and rushed, noiseless in her galoshes, down the deserted back staircase, then out by the French window of the schoolroom to the soaking, slippery lawn. Not until she had felt that treacherous ground could she dare to run; cautiously she

---

13. Freshford is a village, formerly a small town, in County Kilkenny.

picked her way to the gravel, and then, like a lapwing, close and swiftly, with long, effortless measure, she ran through the dank heavy-scented avenue, on, on, on—! But as yet no sign of the other runner: no sound nor sight. It was a question only of pace; there was no second path. Her feet fell lightly, but the gravel crunched and flew; sometimes the outpushed branch of an evergreen swept upon her, drenching her neck with its weight of water, but she never glanced aside, only sped on, her gaze plunging afresh with every turn into the grey, moving darkness.

As she turned the final corner, where the gate-lodge sent a dispersing glow through the atmosphere, there at last was Emily. The splashing of the gravel under their feet deafened each for the noise of the other's progress; Emily kept the uneven measure that was hers in running—a rush for a second or two, then a relapse to an unsteady walk: Elizabeth, going as it were by mechanism, could gain on her now with every breath she drew. And Emily, coming nearer to the lodge, swerved on to the grass of the border: there she could run without noise, though of necessity more heedfully—but as the clash of her own flight ceased upon the gravel, the sound of the pursuit came to her ears. She turned over her shoulder a terrified face, and seeing herself discovered, made a desperate effort, doubled her pace—her foot slid immediately far before her on the sodden earth; she retrieved herself cleverly, but in the second's check Elizabeth had reached her side.

"Emmie!" the elder sister panted, catching at the wet little hand which clasped an impeding skirt. "Emmie dear, thank God I've overtaken you!"

The child wrenched herself away; one moment she stood, defiant, before her captor, then, "You spy—you spy!" she muttered thickly, and sprang forward to renew her flight.

But again Elizabeth caught her, and this time held her. "Call me what you like," she said. "At least I am in time."

"For what?"

"Emmie dear, you know.... Look!"

The gate, pushed open very gently, let in a tall muffled figure, which came towards the two so cautiously that even to them, watching him, his approach was quite inaudible.

"Well, Emmie? Little slowcoach!" he began in a half-laughing voice. "Well? ... By God! Miss Bolton?"

He stopped, completely at a loss, then sharply asked, "A trick, Emmie?"

"Spying!" she flung out. "The spy of the family—the sweet, Christian spy!"

Heaton looked at Elizabeth.

She did not wince. "A spy, if you like, Major Heaton." She turned to her sister. "Emmie you don't know what I know. It's only a little while that I have known it. I didn't like to tell you—I wish now I had. Major Heaton is married."

The word left Emily's demeanour unchanged.

"You must come back with me," Elizabeth said, and waited, unmoved, through the silence that fell and lasted. It was Heaton who first spoke.

"Yes, Emmie. You see, spies have always the pull over the other kind of people. We must give it up." He had lost none of his assurance with Elizabeth's announcement. "Good night, little one." He stood, immensely tall in the spectral atmosphere—made, by his cool reception of the disclosure, more romantic, more glorious even than before in the eyes of Emily.

She tore herself from Elizabeth's hand—was in his arms, gazing up. "Oh, Louis, Louis, I don't care. Oh, let us go! Let me go with you!"

Heaton looked at the sister from above the little panting form, folded an arm about it, made a slight movement towards the gate....

Elizabeth smiled at the bravado. "You know you will not take her now," she said.

His face, by the flare of its angry eyes, the quick display of teeth in the snarl of its lips, lit the gloom as if with lighting for a second—but he relinquished his hold of Emily.

"Spies, as I said, have the advantage," he murmured. "We can do nothing, little one; you must go back—with your sister."

"I won't go back with her," the treble voice insisted. "I will never speak to her again. I wish she was dead."

Heaton bent over her once more. "Child!" he whispered, "we *can't* do anything now. We must make another occasion—we will. But now there's only one thing to be done: you must go back. I'll write and arrange something."

"I won't go back," she repeated; and he, confounded for the instant, caught himself searching with his eyes for aid from the elder girl. At the infuriating consciousness, his anger flamed into speech.

"Go back to the house, Miss Bolton," he said. "You can do nothing more. I will bring your sister to the terrace." His voice had the biting cruelty of a master's to an insolent servant. "You need not fear—you've been most successful as a lady detective."

Elizabeth still wore her ironic smile. "You will follow me directly," she said. "I know that." She turned to go.

Emily strained at once towards the gate. "Let us come, Louis!"

But he was wearying of the scene, with its discomfort, its absurdity of defeat. "No, child. It's utterly useless. You must come back."

She at last allowed him to lead her up the avenue to the terrace, where Elizabeth had stopped again. Aware of the completeness of her advantage, the elder girl had not once looked back nor lingered; but now there was something to be said.

"I will leave the French window in the schoolroom open. It's nearly eight, Emmie, you'll just have time to dress." She passed on, noiselessly, into the house.

... This moment of being left alone with Emily! A vague sense of obligation had impelled Heaton to permit it, but he had dreaded its arrival; and now that it had come, it was still more painful than he had feared. For such a storm of reckless fury as it was, he had not dreamed of as possible from a woman of her upbringing. He shuddered, listening to invectives, epithets, from the childish lips which he would have been disgusted with himself for using: how had she learnt them? And then to utter them! ... It needed to-night's experience to show him that he had indeed some illusions left; earlier in the evening, he would have insisted upon his perfect cynicism—but, good heavens, this was beyond belief! That she scarcely knew what she was saying, he realised: it did not redeem the moment, for the horror was that even her mania could so express itself. His own anger was violent—yes; yet inevitably too he was repelled by Emily's callousness to the disclosure of his design upon her. There were women in whom such an abandonment might have been the crowning glory—women who would have measured their leap with the clear and blinded eyes of passion, who would have seen, undaunted, the end in the beginning; but of these he knew that Emily was not. In her, he divined the mere folly of a curious child; the apparent trust in him was in reality not trust at all, only a vain, absurd belief in her own unending attraction. And besides, he had not told her: he had acted an atrocious part. Strangest revelation! conceiving her as the "little girl"— the unreasoning white ignorance of man's (even cynical man's) inveterate delusion—Heaton had been entirely ruthless; it amazed him to find that now, listening to an utterance of whose rarity he was still convinced—that *now* he should recognise his scheme in all its baseness and its evil!

This was of course his last sight of her. She must not suspect that it was so; but, immutably, so it was. And, standing thus, drenched with the streaming, rustling rain on the death-cold grass, Heaton was aware of nothing in his feeling for her but an ever-increasing dislike.

Was it over? Yes; she had thrown herself, worn out at last, across his grimly folded arms. He supposed he must unfold them!

By promises and caresses whose insincerity he marvelled that she did not feel, he at length induced her to leave him; and while she went stumbling over the lawn to the window, he, with a sigh of relief that reached her romantically as one of desolation, turned instantly and hastened, in the curtain of the rain, down the resonant avenue to the carriage.

The driver was too wet and too sulky to interest himself in the return of his fare; and the unglanced-at Heaton, giving his orders from the window for a dash to save the mail, smiled sardonically to himself as he lay back, alone, in the mouldy cab.

"What a mystery it will grow to, amongst them all. The baffled villain that I am!" His amusement broke into a short, irrepressible chuckle. "I shouldn't be surprised if in time it turned into a legend."

Driscoll, waking again at the sound of the heavy splash and rumble, proved by his watch that the thing had been there for the last twenty minutes, begorra!

"Is it promenading they are, in the fine moonlight it is! Or is it an elopement? Faix,[14] it'd be the very moral of a night, with the dark and the racket of it."

"Elopement or not," Mrs. Driscoll philosophically observed, "'tis off they are. And glory be to God for it, if it'll stop your tongue. Did ye think it'd be one of the young ladies, now, that'd be making a runaway match?"

Driscoll was at last annoyed by her mockery. "Sure, 'twas ye that nursed them. 'Tisn't much of the notion of coortin' that'd be put into them. Didn't I take compassion on ye at the last minute? 'Tis old maids they'll be, the two of them, I tell ye this night. Divil a young gentleman comes next or nigh the place; 'tmight as well call itself a convent and be done with it."

"Sure there's the Major—isn't he after Miss Emily?" the woman said feebly, in defence of her nurslings from the dreadful prophecy.

---

14. An interjection, adapted from "faith".

"Och!" was Driscoll's pregnant comment.

III

Even Heaton, solitary and sardonic, driving back to Freshford in the vehicle of his intended abduction, scarcely supplied a more ironical example of the comedy of life than did Emily, dressing with feverish haste for dinner in the room she shared with Elizabeth, and muttering to herself, the while, an indictment of Desertsurges that closely resembled Driscoll's. She had at first intended not to appear that evening; then the necessity of changing her soaked garments had turned her purpose—she had resolved to brave it out, to go down and let Elizabeth see how little she cared. Moreover, she was far too keenly excited for a breakdown; she could not keep still, she could not keep silent even in her solitude. So, whispering loudly to herself of her hatred for her sister and her home, Emily began the business of dressing.

It promised to demand some energy for its timely accomplishment. Her hair was dripping, the fringe upon the forehead flattened out of all reminiscence of curliness. That had first to be twisted into curling-pins, and the longer hair rearranged; she went about the task as deftly as on any other evening, and was not long in presenting the quaint aspect of a woman *en papillotes*[15]—now made the more comic by her angry and preoccupied expression. In truth, this added to the comedy a touch at first of the merest farce: Emily, with the countenance almost of a fury, going through the complicated little ceremony of dressing, was a spectacle hardly to be excelled in drollery. The hundred tiny businesses—from the pulling off and on of stockings, the choosing of shoes, to the final combing out of the loosened curls and the arranging of gown and ornaments—all were done with an aloofness so complete and passionate that in the end it took something of sinister suggestion. In its automatism, its

---

15. *En papillotes* describes a way of hair styling whereby curls are created by rolling the hair around a piece of paper.

detachment, it seemed to hint at the possibility of madness which lies in every one.

The gong sounded, and she was ready. Its clangour awakened her for other claims: the everyday noise imposed at once the everyday silences—the innumerable, instinctive silences of even the most limpid lives and characters. Emily's tiny reticences were as countless as are every one's: thus she had no tremors before the need for concealment—since she could keep one secret, she could keep all. And indeed, as she entered the drawing-room, there was not perceptible any trace of the recent tempest. Elizabeth was far more unusual in appearance—for, dressed as she had been for dinner before her flight to the rescue, her gown was disarranged, her hair was moistened out of neatness, the fringe clung lankly, the loosened sides had lost their springing fulness, and at the back a wisp hung out over the necklace, forlornly, unbecomingly.

Emily saw it all. With the proof of her greater skill in dissembling, there came to her further aid an audacious malice. She glanced at her sister and said coolly, "You been out, Bessie? Your hair's all wet, as flat as a pancake!" She laughed. "I don't think I should quite care for a stroll *this* evening." Her blue eyes sparkled with excitement and the remnant of her anger.

Elizabeth gasped. "My hair won't keep in curl lately," she faltered, patting and lifting the disordered sides. "It gets like this in wet weather."

Mrs. Bolton ("Aunt Lou," in a fairly good temper) examined her discontentedly. "You do look untidy," she observed. "Why don't you arrange it in some other way?"

The gong broke forth in its final appeal, relieving Elizabeth from the stress of reproof; but as Mr. and Mrs. Bolton passed out of the room, the sisters' eyes met for an instant fully and silently—Elizabeth's, dark with resentment; Emily's, no less ireful, but flashing joyfully with the memory of her morsel of revenge.

"Sweet saint!" she whispered, "why don't you tell?"

"I *will*, if you go on like this," Elizabeth curtly answered.

"Do. Why don't you? But it might get me sent away from here, remember; and that would leave you with no one to spy upon—unless you would like to look after the servants?"

Elizabeth pushed past her violently. "I'll tell them as soon as the servants leave the dining-room," she panted, fully roused.

"All right," said the little voice behind her; "tell them, tell them."

"Girls, girls! What are you doing?" Mrs. Bolton called. "Come in at once to dinner.... Elizabeth you need not look so furious because I spoke to you about your hair."

Emily, taking her seat opposite the elder girl, sent a glance from under lowered eyelids at the burning face. "Tell, tell!" she made with silent lips.

The servants moved about, dinner went its smooth and well-served way; Emily chattered, the elders listened and laughed, but Elizabeth strove in vain to shake off her anger. It was very well to know yourself the heroine of the evening, the saviour of the family—but was it thus that heroines were treated? Were they talked down, covertly insulted? Did they submit? Silent she sat through the courses; but when at last the servants left, and the dalliance with fruit and sweetmeats had set in, she lifted her head, and started resolutely:

"Uncle Tom, there is something I must tell you."

Mr. Bolton looked bored. "Well, well? If it's anything unpleasant, can't it wait? Must it be seen to now, done or written?" He took some raisins from the dish. "I'm sure I hope not. And if it needn't, I'd rather wait until the morning."

Emily tossed a raisin into the air and caught it, descending, in her rosy, widely opened lips. "Look, Uncle Tom!"

He laughed. "That's a pretty trick! The latest, Em?"

"Try it. Try it, Aunt Lou." Aunt Lou demurred. Emily played it again successfully. "Try it, Bessie! You're so good at stopping things." Her eyes were blazing with malice. Mr. Bolton, infected with her merriment, was making desperate efforts at raisin-catching; even Aunt Lou was amused and critical; Elizabeth's moment had gone by, and Emily felt that the flower of her revenge had bloomed already.

The remembrance of Elizabeth's disclosure was hardly a remembrance: it had not really taken hold of her. Either it wasn't true at all, or it was so little true that it didn't signify! Assuredly, Emily's innocence had small beauty, charm, or pathos; yet it existed, and was deeper than Heaton now could by any means have been persuaded to believe. She knew more than he could tolerate in a woman of her age and breeding; yet she was, with it all, profoundly unrealising, childish in a word, before the game of which he had taught her something. Impossible for Heaton to see that! By him, as by most men, it was given against a girl for everything when once she had betrayed a morsel of forbidden knowledge.

Thus, for example, in her folly she believed that it was not yet the end between herself and him—and could, upheld by the excitement of her duel with Elizabeth, look forward to an evening not unbearable. After some restless lingering near the drawing-room fire, some tormenting of the cat who throned in long-backed dignity before it, Emily sauntered to the piano, sat down, began to play. Her eyes were glittering; she tossed up an impertinent little profile and jingled away at her mazurka, living through again, as in a near and vivid dream, that scene so recent yet already so unreal—the frantic light, the capture and the angry words, Elizabeth's victory and Heaton's insults ... seeing again the tall and stately figure, the anger and contempt upon the dark, seamed face, and her own small clinging form, with wild eyes, wild words pleading.

She wondered, confidently, how soon he would write or come; and heard above her music the rustling drone of the rain, as in the long, mysterious avenue of Desertsurges and on the lurid road it stealthily obliterated foot-marks, wheel-marks.

The Turret-Room[16] (*Come In*, 1917)

I

As Nellie Burke, coming home, drove up the shabby avenue of Duneera Castle, she saw her two younger sisters, each with a man, turn into the little path that led to the boathouse. They did not see nor hear her; the governess-cart was hidden by the summer leafage, and Nellie was driving so dejectedly that wheels and pony's hoofs made hardly any sound. She watched the four as they went gaily on amid the sunlight and the movement of green branches; it was a June day of precarious loveliness, but the girls, she noted, wore their quite new muslin frocks. That held meaning for her—meant that Geraldine and Kate had known that the two men were coming out this afternoon. They had not "said a word" to Nellie, but had let her go into town after lunch for marketing, and thus return too late.

Nellie was glad of her lateness. Now she could, unmortified, go up to her own room and have her tea there; while if she had arrived before the river-party started, her programme would have been the same, embittered: that was just the difference it made. But Geraldine and Kate were not to blame for this, nor the two men, nor Nellie Burke herself; it was the way things *were*, no more—no less.

Her room was in the turret that looked out upon the river: sole guerdon of her seniority, for the tower-room, Duneera's gem, had always been the firstborn daughter's appanage. It was a pattern maiden's bower—high-set, deep-windowed; a sense of this had doubtless been the cause of its original conferring on "Miss Burke"; but Nellie used to feel, in bitter moods, that *her* tenure rested more securely on the steep dark stairs that led to it, and its own smallness....

---

16. Mayne read this story to members of the Irish Literary Society in Cork on 14 November 1920. An account of the reading was published in *The Irish Book Lover*, 12, 6–7 (Jan./Feb. 1921), p. 87.

She was proud of her room, but not of herself in it; Kate or Gerry would have filled it better, since to a daughter of the house it must belong. The sons had big, discomfortable, but conveniently placed quarters on the ground-floor at the back; Sir William and his Lady were of course in the best rooms on the first floor. These had no view at all, but had space and accessibility. The younger girls, at the back of the first floor, did envy Nellie her high room, but then, as they agreed, they could not possibly have found another *thing* for which to envy her, so it was only fair. "Poor little Nellie," on good days; "horrid little wretch," on bad ones, summed up the attitude of Geraldine and Kate towards her. They intended neither cruelly; the "horrid" meant no more than a sort of physical distaste, when anyone's temper was on edge, for Nellie's plainness. The soldiers and sailors, who were the givers, at Inishlee,[17] of nicknames, called Miss Burke "the Snipe." Geraldine and Kate had found this out, and though it angered them, they could not be blind to its aptness for Nellie's sharp long nose and insignificant pale head. Her general effect of sickliness was not expressed in it, but no nicknames could have brought together all the disabilities of Nellie; so they had agreed that Snipe, although a shame, was awfully good.

Nellie did not know her nickname, but she knew the rest. On some days it was her nose that she most minded; on other days, her hair—perhaps oftenest her hair, for the younger girls had great possessions in that ways. Kate might grumble because hers was red, but look at the lots she had, poor Nellie used to think, as unavailingly she "French-combed" her own limp, thin locks, and reflected that, with Kate's endowment, her own nose would not have seemed to stick out quite so far. *Her* hair was of the sort about which nobody could chaff her, as men did chaff Kate about the splendid tangle that made every hat, no matter how enormous,

---

17. While Inishlee is not a actual Irish town, its name is clearly meant to sound Irish. Given the presence of British soldiers and sailors, it is probably a garrison and naval town, located near the coast.

look as if it were erected on a hidden little spike. One of the sailors had fondly conveyed this fantasy to Kate herself by asking her, on a day, to lend him the pencil that her hat was always sitting on.

"What are you talking about?" said Kate, but Geraldine had instantly perceived. "Kate's hats do look like that," she cried and then they all—the four, since there was ever a man each—rushed to the glass with Kate to see it dawn on her.

"I don't know what you mean," Kate said (she was distinctly slow); "I only know I can't keep this one on. Hullo! My hair's coming down."

"Take 'em both off," her man exclaimed, seizing the occasion of his life (as he afterwards declared) for getting in a good thing; but Kate only drawled without a smile, "How funny!" and took off the hat, while clutched at the crinkly locks and brought them really down.

"They *are* her own!" he cried, and pulled one to full length.

"Well, mightn't you have known it?" Kate said bitterly. "Who'd have false *red* hair?"

"I like your old carrots," said her sailor and kissed the lock, making a wry face, as he finished, that he didn't mean at all—it was only for the others. He did like her old carrots; he very nearly was in love with Kate herself. Not quite; one didn't want to fall in love just yet; and besides, there was Sir Bill....

For Nellie there were not these moments; nor had she the more comic fame of Geraldine's gold hair—luxuriant as Kate's, but with a queer effect of being all ends. The ends were everywhere, and the beginnings nowhere. Men used affectionately to bet about her: would she be tidy to-day? She never was, and Odds-and-Ends became Geraldine's nickname. Kate hadn't any; Carrots was too obvious even for the garrison.

So Nellie was glad she had come home late, not only because she was dusty and shabby, but because whatever she had been, no one would have wanted her. No man ever had. She literally did not know how, if a man ever had, she might have felt about such an expedition. Would she have wished to go alone with "him," or been content, as were the others, to knock about all day in the one boat, chaffing and laughing and singing, and landing only to "rag" more actually with sticks and stones while they made tea? Nellie thought, uncertainly, that she might have wished for different things from these—for long, grave tête-à-têtes with sudden silences and looks, and landings that would bring about a climax to the looks and silences. They would wander in Duneera's woods, it might be hand-in-hand, find wild-flowers and bird's-nests and little singing streams, and look into each other's eyes afresh with each discovery....

Sometimes, in her turret, Nellie would sit dreaming thus; not often, for she was ashamed—ashamed to know that when she should stand up, the glass would show her the sharp nose, the thin pale hair ... ashamed of that, and of some other things besides that were less utterly her own, but *were* her own, as well as Geraldine's and Kate's and the boys', and the mother's.

Nellie would sit shuddering, not dreaming, on "bad" days, or else dreaming of what life might have been like if, though she still were plain, Sir Bill were not the famous drunkard of the place. Sometimes she used to think that she could then have borne to be the plain Miss Burke; sometimes she seemed to know that it would not have made much difference—for if any one had loved her, even as things were, she could perhaps have felt about Sir Bill what all the others felt. That seemed to have become little. Even Lady Burke now took it almost as a matter of course; she had formed it into a kind of routine. Everyone in or about the Castle knew exactly what to do when Sir Bill was brought home on somebody's car, having been found dead-drunk in a ditch, on market-days. On those days Dempsey would keep near the house, so as to be there to take him down and help him to his room; then Lady Burke would be informed.

"Who was it brought Sir William, Dempsey?" she would ask, obeying the melancholy curiosity which, even in her, had superseded grief—but still with dignity, though she was red-faced, ugly, short, with sad blue staring little eyes. "Who was it found Sir William this time?" She would ask it quite spontaneously; "this time" held no bitterness of emphasis; it was just complete acceptance.

"Andy Finnegan, my lady," Dempsey might reply, and then the order would go forth that Andy was to put up his horse and have his tea in the kitchen. Or it might be "Mr. Stuart, my lady"; that would mean the police-officer—the "D.I."—who would have been coming home from Petty Sessions and have found Sir Bill, and done his deed of charity, and fled.[18]

Mr. Stuart would come out, perhaps next day, to tennis at Duneera, and no one would feel shy; it was doubtful, indeed, that anyone would remember—it happened so often. At first Lady Burke had tried, by stoppage of supplies, to cure Sir Bill. She had long controlled the money (what there was of it): at Inishlee it was common talk that Sir Bill never had more than twopence in his pocket on market-days. But what good was that, people used to say compassionately, when every publican in the place would give him credit? and besides there were the endless treatings.... It was *no* good, as Lady Burke had realised; then the routine had been set going, and now there was nothing more to be said or done.

Nellie was apparently the only one who "minded." Duneera that she might have loved seemed so debased by these things, and the worse things which as often happened, that she had grown to hate it. When Sir Bill came home on his own car, for instance, it was worse; for then he would either be alone and in a rage, or would bring with him some comrade or some comrades of the public-houses, "merry" as himself, and they would go into the dining-room, there to sit and drink, until the servants had to make up beds for "the dear knows who" in the spare rooms, while

---

18. D.I. refers to District Inspector, a rank in the Royal Irish Constabulary. A "Petty Session" was the local court of the district that dealt with such matters as minor theft, assault, drunkenness, and arbitration.

Sir Bill was helped to *his* by Dempsey, expert in this if in no other of his duties. To hear the clumping, staggering feet, and the more obscene testimonies to Duneera's hospitality, or the curses that betokened solitary coming-home ... such alternatives explained Andy Finnegan and Mr. Stuart as the mitigation they could be for everyone but Nellie, who, once she reached her turret, was immune. *She* could better bear those ills; for they, when she did hear them, spoke of life as something so appalling that it must one day be different, while the routine, in its comparative seemliness, could and would go on for ever.

"For ever." She was young enough to have that word in her vocabulary. Nellie was twenty-six; Geraldine and Kate were twenty-two and twenty. But Geraldine and Kate would get away—would marry. Not any of these men: the gay, the transient soldiers, or the still more gay and transient sailors—or at any rate, not probably; but there would *be* a man, some day, for Geraldine and Kate. For Nellie, no. People said they liked her best, but that meant little. It meant merely that some women and the older men felt sorrier for her, and would take her part, against her sisters' more light-hearted way of life. But they were seldom so inspired; there was nothing to condemn in either Geraldine or Kate, who were, really, universal favourites. Nellie, in her melancholy and her sickliness and her effacement, was not quite that. Her rare champions knew no more of her than did the rest—the younger soldiers and sailors and their infrequent wives, or those girls with whom her sisters most consorted. But even Geraldine and Kate had few intimates among women. The routine made women shy: "it was so awful to be there when Sir Bill came home." That *had* happened once or twice, and it was difficult for the female order to know what to say or do. Men found the situation easier, because there were the girls and Lady Burke to look after.... So Duneera was becoming a man's house, and no one except Nellie seemed to "mind" that, either.

Nellie sometimes thought she minded everything, sometimes

knew she didn't. Little sudden shocks came on her, like that caused by the man who dropped a coin one day, and went down on his knees to look for it. They were in the drawing-room—the drawing-room with its great view—and it was tea-time. Nellie was there, on that occasion. They all bent down; the coin was not to be discerned—it must have rolled. One of the men raised the frill of a sofa-cover, and laughed loudly, crying out, "I say! Look here." Nellie was nearest, so she looked. Under the sofa was a great pile of "sloven's fur," and Lady Burke's long-missing thimble, and cakes rejected, days and days or weeks and weeks ago, by the dogs, and a chicken's head that one of them had brought in, and ... something unspeakable which betrayed Duneera's equal love for cats. Nellie didn't laugh, but Geraldine and Kate (after an instant) and the men did.

"I say! You'll have to give Nora what-for.... The sovereign may be there. Who's going to feel for it?"

The men's eyes met; amusement and disgust and pity stood in them. Nellie looked at Geraldine and Kate. Though both were laughing still, she saw that both were angry, and ashamed. But what could anybody say or do? To be cross with the men would only make it worse.

Nellie spoke at last. "The room shall be thoroughly turned out to-morrow, Mr. Summers. If the sovereign's there, you'll hear from some of us at once." Her voice was gentle, but her pale cheek burned.

The young man who was responsible felt penitent. "Oh no; I couldn't think of giving all that trouble." But as he spoke, he grew aware that he was blundering. "I mean, don't hurry about it; any time will do." He hadn't improved it much! His comrades bit their lips, to hide the smiles. That was one thing. It belonged, in some mysterious way, to all the rest, thought Nellie—the rest that didn't specially concern herself. But then, reflecting further, Nellie felt that this might specially concern herself. She was the plain Burke, the "quiet" one—why didn't *she* look after things like this?

She might do that much! But there was difficulty about servants at Duneera; it was "lonely," the maids found; they couldn't easily get into town, and all the men about the place were married. This was bad; and then there was the endless trouble caused by Sir Bill's habits—the sudden hospitalities to people whom the servants bitterly resented as creatures to be waited on, the everlasting calls for whisky, which often must be answered by wild rushes to the nearest public-house—of course there was a near one. Indulgence, slackness, the blind eye, were more imperative at Duneera even than elsewhere in Ireland; when the Burkes got hold of a girl who was in any way capable—and Nora could do some things—much art was exercised to keep her. Should Nellie interfere with her, attempt to scold her, for example (in the timid fashion that was Nellie's), about an exposure like to-day's, there would be instant "notice," and the weary search to do again. Though Nellie would do that, as she did always, she knew that it would mean but scant improvement, and the long troubled period, first, of getting the new housemaid "used" to Sir Bill's ways.

The sofa episode hurt Nellie mortally. There were some things she didn't notice then, and one of them was dirt. She had lived on, placidly, in squalor such as that; she had even been rather proud of the drawing-room. Perhaps the visitors had always noticed it; it might be another of the jokes about Duneera. Mr. Summers hadn't seemed to be surprised; it was more as if he had thought they knew and didn't care. Or perhaps he meant it for a friendly hint. People might have found the atmosphere so awful that a "pal" had seized the occasion to say something. Did the drawing-room *smell*, and hadn't the Burkes noticed that, either?

Nellie cried, that day, when she escaped to her own room. The liquid pale-brown eyes, when she had finished crying, looked out upon the river desolately, and saw the others, drifting, laughing, just as usual.... The room was thoroughly turned out next day, and Mr. Summers' gold coin was found under the very sofa. Kate wrote him a note to say so; he came and got the sovereign. Did they laugh together over its retrieval, Nellie wondered. Kate had said, on the evening of the dreadful day, that he'd been horrid, but the only thing to do was not to seem to mind. Geraldine agreed—so did Nellie, for that matter. But Nellie had tacked on a comment.

"How *can* you like him, Kate?"

"I don't care a ha'porth about him," Kate said lightly, in her pretty brogue.

"Then why do you ask him out so often?"

"Oh, don't bother, Nellie. We've been over that ground often enough, haven't we?"

They had. It was the eternal question of "what else is there to do?"; and Nellie felt that she was a poor champion of her side of it. Nobody could want to live like her, neglected by the Mr. Summerses and Winters, lonely every way, as idle as the rest, and never getting any fun at all. If she had been clever, if she had even been religious.... They all went into Inishlee for church on Sundays—the Protestant church, for this branch of the Burkes had somehow become Protestant. Their pew was in a splendid place, the front one in the northern transept; it commanded the military pew opposite, where the officers of the church-party from the Barracks sat. Whether that pew was full or half empty depended on the regiment which happened to be garrisoning Inishlee at any given time. Should it be, territorially speaking, an "English" one, the pew was full, for then a greater number of the men would be of the "Protestant" faith, and so there were, naturally, more officers required to bring them to church. An Irish or Scottish regiment meant a half-empty pew. Just now it was an English one, and the party was so large that the band came with it—there was almost a formal church-parade. The band was good, as such bands go; Inishlee thought it magnificent; scarlet coats and glittering helmets blazed in the grey square before the old and lovely church (once the Catholic Cathedral); on fine days, all girls wore best frocks and hats, and those were better ones than usual when the regiment at Inishlee was English. When service was over, you met the officers coming out. The church-party would be forming up, and your man was perhaps for a while unconcerned in that manoeuvre. It was nice to be saluted, instead of having a mere hat taken off to you; your man turned into a higher order of being, yet was still your man, and all the more so for the vanity of his calling, which—no girl could help noticing—still survived in even the most senior when he met her and conversed with her, in uniform. The self-consciousness—girls called it conceit—thus induced in him enhanced her own; she almost trembled, she quite blushed; it was the best of all the meetings, though so short, for soon his duty would remove him, and the band blared out, and "They" marched off resplendent, leaving happy hearts behind, and eyes that sparkled brighter even than on other days, lit by the tumult of the beating quick-step, with its insolence that was so gay, its heartlessness that was so manly.

Yes: they went to church on Sundays. Even Nellie sometimes had a gorgeous man to talk to, for the Burkes, despite Sir Bill, were personages, and looked-out-for. When there wasn't a big party and the band, there were still the scantier units—there was sure to be some fun; but on those more concentrated days, Miss Burke returned to her background, and saw church with an undazzled eye. On such days, she saw that church was not *religion*. What was religion? Nellie did not know, and could not have found out. Nobody she knew was religious—for she knew not many Catholics, and those she did know never talked about their faith. It is not, for various reasons, one of the things done in Ireland, among the class to which the Burkes and their acquaintances belonged. The outward gestures of the national faith were, naturally, familiar to her: the servants went to confession (and a great nuisance it was to arrange for); there were Lady-days and Saints' Days, and the Friday fast—another nuisance, for fish was hard to get, out at Duneera. In the season boys came round with salmon-peel—poached of course from the famed river, Inishlee's great "sight," that shows to gasping visitors the sensational silver clumps ("Good God! and those are *salmon!*") lying thickly under and beyond a bridge in the very middle of the town.... But you couldn't afford salmon, even at poached prices, for the kitchen dinner; and the servants would complain, at regular intervals, of the eternal salted ling.

The parish priest dined at Duneera sometimes. He was not impressive. Even the remarkable Father Lally, of Inishlee itself, lost value when he came to the Castle. What he was remarkable for was precisely his temperance work. That was difficult to talk of, with Sir Bill at the head of a table.... Their own clergyman took people like themselves for granted, though he too was famous for his zeal, and was besides a noted preacher—you could really listen to his sermons. Nellie did; but they, like everybody's sermons, began at a point of fervour which she had never reached.

She did no good works. Few girls do, in Ireland, and (as in most lands) never they who do the more amusing things. Though Nellie didn't do those very much, she belonged, by all the circumstances of her life, to that division, and her delicacy, with its consequent inertia, made another reason. There was nothing, in short, that she could turn to; Nellie just existed, vaguely. That is Ireland, for girls of her calibre.

II

The turret-room, remote and high, cut off from the house proper by its little door, could sometimes seem a refuge, but could sometimes frighten her. The little door was frightening, for it stuck, and had to be much pulled and shaken from her side, before she could get out.... One night last winter, when the elders were away and the boys dining at the Barracks, Nellie had come into the drawing-room crying. Geraldine and Kate were startled, but they soothed her tears, and she said apologetically, when she could stop sobbing: "I was only thinking—suppose there was a fire some night! That awful door...."

They laughed. "The devil looks after his own."

"I'm not his own," said Nellie, brokenly.

"I meant the house," said Geraldine, in a rare tone of bitterness.

"Do you—*mind* too then, Gerry?"

"What's the good of minding? A short life and a merry one."

"Is it merry?" Nellie quavered.

Kate frowned on her. "The Burkes were never grousers, anyhow, so don't let *us* begin."

"Grousing's no worse than disgracing the house we live in, and that's what these Burkes do—'the oldest baronet in Ireland's family!' I wish Duneera would fall down," said Nellie in her dim voice, slowly, with no vehemence at all. Her brogue was marked as she spoke thus: that is the way with Irish gentry, when moved deeply.

"It won't, then, so keep your horrid wishes to yourself. Can't you be proud of the old place, instead of abusing it?"

"It's us I'm abusing," Nellie said. "But indeed I'm not proud of Duneera; I hate the sight of it, going to rack and ruin the way it is, and ourselves with it. I'd be thankful if it fell down and was buried in the ground, every stone of it, and then perhaps we might lead decent lives, out of this." She spoke in the same monotone, coloured only by the Irish inflections.

"It's like a curse on the place," murmured Kate; but Geraldine, as usual, was quicker to understand.

"She's only frightened. Why don't you change into one of the downstairs rooms, Nellie?"

"I will, I think. But there'd be such a fuss; they'd imagine the world was coming to an end. It's only in the winter I mind it, with that awful door, and the wind howling down the stairs behind me and putting out the candle, the way it did to-night."

Gerry shivered. "I don't know how you stand it." But the plan of changing to another room got put off and put off, in native fashion; the weeks and months went by, and Nellie slept behind the little door, and the door stuck.... Now it was the summer;

terrors fade on summer nights. Nellie, on this afternoon of late home-coming, rejoiced to think she hadn't changed her room—the view had never looked more lovely, never solaced her so much. There was something in the sunlit river, flowing by, that promised tranquillity; nothing that she could define, but the dim soul in her was drawn on to some vaguely figured end that should be like the river's—what she wanted or what she must yield to? Nellie didn't know; enough that it would come—the quiet, perhaps the glad, attainment—no less for her than for the river.

Sitting in the window, dreaming so, she saw her sisters and their men come in, and only then perceived that the bright day had clouded over. A rough wind had blown up from the sea; "all the way from America," as people say of the west wind at Inishlee. Nellie stayed in her own room till dinner-time; not till then were the guests gone. Dinner rarely waited for Sir Bill; it would not wait to-night, for this was a great day in Inishlee. The Land Leaguers[19] of an outlying district had been turbulent; several were "up" at Petty Sessions there, and Sir Bill, as a J.P. of the County, had driven over to take his place on the bench.[20] Inishlee was foaming with excitement—Nellie had seen something of it during her shopping—about the Leaguers and the presence in their district (later to be looked for in the county-town itself) of one of the most impassioned Nationalist Members.[21] It was rumoured that he was to be arrested, that night in Inishlee; there was sure to be disturbance if he were.... On such occasions the uncertain "state

---

19. The Irish National Land League was a political organisation that campaigned for land reform in the final two decades of the nineteenth century. They sought to curb the power of landlords and campaigned for the rights of tenant farmers.
20. Part of the British legal system, a J.P. or Justice of Peace served on the bench under supervision of resident magistrates at petty sessions to try minor offences and under supervision of a county court judge to try more serious offences at quarter sessions.
21. The phrase probably refers to a prominent member of the Irish National Land League, which was also in support of the nationalist cause in Ireland.

of the country" faded, even for the inured women of Duneera, before the certain state of Sir Bill, who was a rabid Unionist.[22] When to all the rest of the reasons for getting into that state was added this, of having to drink destruction to the foes of Imperial Unity ... it was worse than market-day; if he did come home accompanied, the party would be "farther gone," and would go on still farther, than on ordinary nights; there was no hope at all of the routine.

The boys were absent too, in case there should be any fun, so the Duneera ladies dined alone. None of them was interested in the wider issue; Unionist women of their class, in all parts of Ireland but Ulster, show a detachment from the Question[23] which, originating in native irony, is fed, in cases like the Burkes', by a near view of Unionism as represented by the Sir Bills and their adherents.... So dinner was depressing, and the hour afterwards was worse. Rain had ceased, but the great wind was getting up and up; the girls could not go out, and the long summer-twilight made things inexpressibly forlorn. They sat in the drawing-room a while, restlessly, then they prepared for bed. No one would wait up for the men; it was impossible to guess when any of them might arrive.

"Even the boys will be squiffy to-night," said Geraldine, who cultivated slang.

"Oh, Gerry, not the boys—they never are," cried Nellie.

"That's all *you* know about it, away up there in your turret!"

"Thank goodness I am, then," she retorted, but the boast died in her heart as she went up, her candle flickering in the gusts that

---

22. In opposition to Nationalists, Unionists supported the parliamentary union between Great Britain and Ireland. In a letter of 1 August 1924 to Macgillivray, Mayne refers to herself as a nationalist: "as soon as I came to years of discretion, [I] was always on the Nationalist side. My sister, too—and she has married into a family more truly Irish than the Maynes; her husband (also a British soldier; a gunner, now retired) is a Cotter, but both my brothers are 'Unionists'—that obsolete sect!"

23. "The Irish Question" was the phrase used by the British to refer to the cause of Irish nationalism and independence.

whirled through at the eyelet-windows. The dark stairs rustled as the dust and leaves on them were stirred; drear echoes whimpered in the background—Nellie was unstrung and nervous by the time she reached her room. She stood a moment, covering her face; then went to the window to look out upon the grey lift of the river, flowing strong and fast. Again it calmed her; she undressed, and read a while in bed to reassure herself still further—Edna Lyall;[24] Nellie loved her. Then she put out her light and fell asleep, despite the storm.

It seemed a long time afterwards that she was standing in the dark, without a candle, at the little door, and it was stuck, and she was pulling it and calling. She strove to wake, and woke, and it was not a dream. In the house there were strange noises, and the wind was higher than before. The noises grew in number and in violence; footsteps would sound near one moment, and she called more hopefully, but they had not been near, and they were gone, and the voices that had cried were fading. In the darkness she tugged on at the stiff door; it did not loosen, and through it there came drifting in the smoke that made her cough, and little flames were creeping under it—the only things that she could see. She saw them, and she felt the smoke possess her throat; as in a nightmare pang her breath went from her, and now another pain began, in one foot, where the flames were creeping in—she caught the long white nightdress and clutched it round her, tugging at the door again with that restricted reach. Beyond it, on the other side, was a dull gathering roar that sounded like the kitchen boiler when it got too hot; and Nellie listened and she shrieked—"I'm here, Mamma, Mamma—Kate, Geraldine—Mamma, I'm here"—and listened, and ran back to the dark stairs and set one foot on them, but then ran back again and sobbed between her screams, for now there was no sound at all but the dull roar and the wind rushing down the stairs behind her through the eyelet-windows. The door

---

24. Edna Lyall is the pen name of Ada Ellen Bayly, a very popular English novelist in the late-Victorian period.

was driven back each time it seemed to loosen; the wind found out the little flames; they shot up into the smoke, but the door gave at last, and through it walked a sheet of fire, tall, strong, and splendid, and it met the strong wild wind, and both embraced her as a man might have embraced, and into those two arms she sank, and called and sobbed no more. They held her close until she lay within them, not as she had been when she was born—no, not like that; like nothing that you could have known for her, nor for a woman's body, nor for anything at all.

Upon the lit, blown lawn the others huddled shivering in their night-attire.... It seemed not so very strange.... Sir Bill, a powerful big man, was not undressed, nor were his "friends," who this time numbered four. They were all sober now, though they had been more drunk than ever when the first shriek sounded, and the household seemed to tumble helter-skelter into the dark hall that was no longer dark, but bright with a wide throbbing glimmer that grew wider every instant. Sir Bill's party was sitting in the dining-room without a light, for not a candle had been left for him—there was nothing but a fixed lamp on the first-floor landing, and the oil in that was sinking low. Sir Bill had been beside himself with rage: "It had been done on purpose to disgrace him before his friends," and he had stamped down into the kitchen, dropping matches on his way, to find the necessary glasses, and prove to the bemused quartette that he was master in his own house.

Now, through the half-open door, they saw the women in the hall. Sir Bill got up and staggered out; he stood there in the pulsing light, not asking what it was, but swearing at the women for their "row" and the forgotten candles. He stopped and stared, in a few seconds—his throat was full of something, and he looked around more angrily than ever, as if to ask what this new trick might be. A glittering tongue of flame leaped forth to answer; he seemed to sober on the instant.... the whole night-gowned company of women was running to the door before the shepherding five men ... and then they were all out upon the lawn, and Duneera streaming like a banner into the dim sky of coming day.

A woman's voice shrilled suddenly above the roar of storm and fire.

"Great God Almighty, where's Miss Nellie?"—and Dempsey, the same instant, ran up from the river-path. His cries were tossed upon the wind as he came onward.

"Miss Nellie's in the turret, and it roaring like the sea with flames and burning! Holy Mother of God, I heard her voice, and she calling in the turret—aye, hearken, my lady, it's for you and the young ladies she's calling, but sure nobody could go into the place. My God, what will we do; she's well-nigh consumed by now, and she crying and calling the whole time, so it'd lacerate your soul to hear her—"

"Ah, go to hell with your soul and your talk out of that," Sir Bill screamed savagely, and ran to the turret-path, while all around broke forth a wailing from the women-servants, and Lady Burke fell on her knees and beat her hands upon the grass, her grey hair blowing feebly in the wind. Geraldine and Kate stood, clasping one another, for a second, then together fled towards Nellie's path, but Sir Bill ran back and Dempsey followed them; they were seized and held, and while they struggled and cried out that "somebody must save her," Dempsey, holding Geraldine with hands that never loosened, said in a quick quiet voice, most strange to hear from him who had so babbled but a moment since, "Ah, look at that, miss," and they looked, to see the turret flare from every eyelet, quiver, break in two, the lower part collapsing on itself, while the crest fell with a loud clatter of wide-leaping stones upon the path and lawn.

An hour afterwards they still stood in a haggard group beside the place where it had been. The fire brigade had come at last, but Duneera too was fallen in a heap of flickering stones; and there was nothing for the men to do but play their hose upon the smaller mound, that so, in time, they might find Nellie there. With every minute that the household watched, the terror of that small mound's secret seemed to deepen.... Dempsey, standing at the back with other servants, suddenly caught Nora's arm. She had tossed up her head in a strange gesture, like a baying dog's.

"Keep quiet, girl!"

She turned on him; her eyes were shining with a wild clear light. He gripped her arm more urgently.

"For all sakes, keep quiet. They think to find her corpse, and she in that place till it melted! But how could they be thinking of it the way we can, and she their own that they forgot, God help them?"

"If they find annything itself," another man said, dully, "what one of them would be able to say it was Miss Nellie and not the rest of the rubbish? I've heard tell how bones can be consumed to ashes."

At this, the girl threw up her head again, but Dempsey covered her mouth quickly with his other hand.

"For the love of God, keep quiet.... Never fear but you'll get your chance—"

"Aye, wait so," the other man joined in. "Sure when was there a funeral went out of the Castle but your family was at it, since th'ould days when the Burkes were Catholics? Faith, they never forgot them days, for all they turned."

"And what funeral would go out this time?" the girl, freeing her lips with a wild movement, interrupted. "That'll be a quare funeral without a corpse—the quarest my family ever went to, I'm thinking and they the greatest in all Connaught for the keening-women.[25] Is it an empty coffin ye'd have them keen, Peter Dempsey and John Meehan, that ye have that talk out of ye?"

The men turned pale. "Begob, she's right," said Dempsey in an awestruck whisper. "I hadn't the sense to make it out like that."

"'Tis truth; she's in the right," Meehan agreed. "And Miss Nellie the first young girl ever died at Duneera, for all the rest was married women."

---

25. Keening is a vocal lament for the dead, a Gaelic tradition in Ireland and the prerogative of women.

"What will they do at all, the creatures, when it comes on them the way it did on you and me?" But Dempsey, in his recognition of her "sense," had forgotten Nora's dread inheritance. She raised her head again in the strange dog-like gesture, he caught her arm again: "Keep quiet!" but the girl, now shaken to the soul, was past restraint—she uttered the unearthly cry; it pierced the shuddering dawn, and Sir Bill turned, with a quick face of terror, then dropped upon the ground beside the heap of stones, and cursed her kneeling.

"Stop that howling bitch, you fools—clap your hand on her mouth and smother her. Damn her and all the Clancys and their screeching women! Can't you wait for the funeral, you—"

"What funeral?" she moaned, as if the words were in the eldritch chant; then, breaking off her cry: "'Tis now ye'll have Miss Nellie keened or never, or will ye bury the whole place with her that ye may get her bones blest that way? No other way will ye contrive it, if ye were looking till the Judgment Day—and may the Holy Powers forgive you on that day, Sir William Burke of Duneera, to be miscalling me and my family that has the knowledge of the keening, and it come down to them since ever there was a Burke at the Castle—aye, and before it, and you cursing them on your knees beside the place that'll be Miss Nellie's only grave—"

But the other servants, spellbound until now, were on her, and though once more the keen swelled, rising, falling, on the sunless dawn, she suffered them to lead her down the drive to the gate-lodge; and all along the road to Inishlee the people woke to hear the death-cry from Duneera, and rush, terror-struck, to learn from those who now came towards them from the Castle, "what was it happened to the Burkes."

III

The Clancy women, in their ceremonial hooded cloaks, were waiting on a misty morning, two days later, at the Castle gates. Nora was among them, hooded too; she was to "have her chance," for Dempsey had been right—Sir Bill had reverenced old custom. The Clancy tradition dated with the Burkes' first records; he had sent the awaited summons to the famous keening-women.

They stood, faceless in the falling hoods, and murmured to each other.

"'Tis madness, but what else would ye expect?"

"Sure how did annyone ever get such a notion?"

"'Twas Nora put it in his head."

"'Twas so. That very night I said it, and himself cursing me the whole time."

"And the Protestant clergyman to let him—but that's the way with Protestants, they can do what they like."

"Ah, Sir William Burke's a big man amongst the quality, for all he's half disgraced. 'Twas that did it, and not the religion at all. What one of them at the Castle ever had the name of religion? Miss Nellie herself, and she a quiet little thing, was never that way, and not one of the rest would annyone be considering. Her Ladyship lost heart; she was no more than the shadow of a woman, this long time."

"My brother passed that remark this morning. 'How particular he is about the burying,' says he; 'him that never cast a thought on them things all his life till now!'"

"'Consecrated ground' is the name they have for it, and would ye ever think to see such a thing as that, to be burying the whole place in the Protestant graveyard with Miss Nellie, for fear they wouldn't know which was her and which was the Castle?"

"Arrah, what else would they do?" cried Nora. "Would ye have them cart away her dust and ashes with the rubbish? 'Tis only the little turret, moreover, will be buried—so let ye keep quiet, and not have so much talk between yourselves. He's a fine solemn man, when he's sober; only for the red face of him and a taint of whisky on the breath, no one'd think since Miss Nellie was burnt that he ever raised his elbow at all.... Whisht! They're coming. Now let ye be quiet and myself'll raise the keen, for that's my certain due that lived in the same house with her."

The hooded women drew together, like a chorus, as from the house there came the funeral group. A vast coffin swayed upon the bearers' shoulders; its gathered contents, firmly packed by scandalised experts, seemed to the Duneera men a burden incommensurate with human fortitude. They had been carefully rehearsed by the undertakers, but now that they were carrying, no more a simulacrum, but the very thing itself, each face was rigid, haunted—they were "mutes" indeed. As they moved onward, now and then they thought to hear a grinding of the stones against each other—the stones among which crept the dust that was and was not Nellie.... At any moment panic might have seized them; but they came on with their set faces where the eyes alone had life, and that the life of terror as they glanced, at intervals, beneath the bristling box to one another.

Sir Bill, pale, solemn, under the grotesque stigmata of his normal life, came close behind with Lady Burke. She was indeed but "the shadow of a woman" in her black envelopment, faceless as the hooded chorus, and with no such outlet for the awe that wrapped her like her clinging veil. The boys were next—two fair-haired, puzzled creatures, vexed by the eccentric, sullen in a sense of make-believe. Geraldine and Kate went hand-in-hand; their faces, just discernible in less obliterating masks than Lady Burke's, were like the coffin-bearers', tranced with terror. Each held more tightly to the other's hand, as every step drew on to that with which the women's wailing would break out—the keen that they had heard of all their lives, but never heard in its full ceremonial meaning until now. Their souls were shuddering from that, as they had shuddered from the rest of the dread burying that ground the little dust beneath its ghastliness.

"And she that hated the whole place!"

"She wished it would fall down and bury itself...."

So, with shaken hearts, the sisters, when they heard of it, had whispered to each other. The irony for which they had no name confounded them; they felt they knew not what. But they came meekly on behind the symbol of her final impotence—it reached the gate, and now, with such a sound as mocks imagination, Nora's solitary cry received it. The coffin quivered on the bearers' shoulders—they stopped short, but with a muttered invocation ("Holy Virgin, guard her soul!") they braced themselves again. The hooded women turned to walk beside; each joined in while she turned, and the blank sky might seem to curdle as the waves of human woe poured into it.

The Happy Day (*Blindman*, 1919)

The town was dirty, stately, comic, and morose—quite Irish, they said. Broken little bridges took you over nothing; there had once been a canal and now there wasn't. But the horse-fair still flourished, and something else was going on besides—a religious festival, they gathered, for sudden small processions met them, and at corners there were knots of little girls in starched white muslin and blue ribbons, with white cotton stockings and black sturdy boots that had brass lace-holes, and the laces had brass tags. Most of the little girls had thin waved hair that stood out weakly under veils of cheap stiff muslin, and betrayed each stricture of the plaits it had been in the night before. And it was more like tow than hair, for nearly all the little girls were blonde. This vexed the visitors, for they had come with preconceived ideas, and one was that the women of all ages in the "Irish" parts of Ireland had black rich hair, and blue or deep-grey eyes in pallid faces that were sad or scornful. "Cathleen-ni-Houlihan":[26] that was the note; the beauty

---

26. Cathleen ni Houlihan is the main character of a one-act play written by William Butler Yeats and Lady Gregory of the same title. It premiered in 1902 with Maud Gonne as leading actress. The play became very popular in London in the first decade of the twentieth century. More generally, Cathleen ni Houlihan is seen as a nationalist symbol for Ireland, inspiring young men to lay down their life for their country.

of the Irish Players' leading actresses had stressed it.[27] London was cured of the Colleen[28]—she was only fit for cinemas and postcards; but there had to be a type, as with all foreign lands, so Dark Rosaleen was now enthroned in their imaginations[29].... And behold, these little wax-doll girls, conspiring in a blissful insipidity at every corner!

"*Enfants de Marie,*"[30] Felicia yawned, though it was Ireland; but she had been eternally in France, and never before in Ireland, so her comments came forth in the tongue most natural to her when sight-seeing. "Isn't this Assumption Day or something—the fifteenth of August?"

---

27. In 1902 the National Irish Theatre Association first performed *Cathleen ni Houlihan* in Dublin, and later also in London.
28. Colleen is an Irish English word for girl, derived from the Gaelic *cailín*. It may also refer to the play *The Colleen Bawn* (1860) by the Irish-born playwright Dion Boucicault. After a successful career in London, Boucicault moved to the U.S., where he started writing plays that were explicitly Irish in setting and characters. The first of these was *The Colleen Bawn*, which was "hugely successful", notes Anthony Roche, and "brought Boucicault back in triumph to the London stage" (Roche 2015, 10).
29. "Dark Rosaleen" is the title of a nationalist poem by James Clarence Mangan. It is another, more outspokenly nationalist, female figure used to represent Ireland. The opposition with the "colleen" implied in this passage refers to two different female complexions that were considered typical for Ireland: reddish-brown hair with a freckled face vs. black hair with a pale complexion. The English tourists find neither in Ireland, for the girls they meet are blonde. That the colleen has been replaced by Dark Rosaleen may also hint at the fact that Boucicault's melodramas abruptly fell out of favour in the late nineteenth century, not only because of the new success of Yeats and Gregory, but also because "Ireland's increasing struggle for political independence from England made the utopian metaphor and the political allegory of a marriage between the two countries increasingly untenable" (Roche 2015, 14).
30. *Enfants de Marie* literally means "children of Mary", but the phrase refers specifically to young girls who belong to the French Catholic organisation "Enfants de Marie immaculée", founded in 1837 with a view to preparing girls for a religious life. In some of Kate O'Brien's novels there are Irish Catholic women, educated in France or Brussels, who are members of the *Enfants de Marie*, but these girls, who are in their First Communion dresses for the procession on Assumption Day, are unlikely to have been members.

Lant knew what it was—he was a Catholic; but he said nothing, just marched on beside her, very tall and even fairer than the little girls.

The town played-up, at all events. "Worn and torn," she said, achieving English this time.

Lant said: "Why not *morne?*"[31]

He sounded cross. He did jeer at her French sometimes; she spoke it better than he could. If he was cross, she mustn't be. The day seemed setting in for failure; crossness on both sides would be the last stupidity! She'd know if Lant was cross so soon as he said anything that had long words in it. If he didn't finish the long words, but left their ends to float like a spider's threads in his companion's mind, it would be proof that he was not cross. She had marked this as a symptom of good-temper since the earliest days of his love-making. "Captive balloons!" she'd cried; and Lant had been delighted. It was her sort of thing to say, he had remarked; and she had been surprised and pleased, because she did not know she *had* a "sort of thing," and never would—she was so little self-aware. But every time that she was told she had, it pleased her freshly, and she had been told often before Lant began to be the teller-in-chief.

Lant was really Lancelot, but of course that couldn't be endured. He had been Lant before she knew him; she had no desire to alter it. The vulgar ugliness might well be balm to a proud spirit wincing from the vulgar prettiness; and then, in her own way, she savoured it herself. To whisper your love's name and have it Lant appealed to a grim humour in her that was always charmed by the wrong thing of the right sort. Her own name was as bad: Felicia. Lant and Lish would have been exquisite, but she had always been Felicia. Lish was the kind of thing that didn't happen to her, like so many other things; for *her* name had at least one merit—that of irony. Lant had shown her this. He said that she was of the type for whom felicity looms in the offing, almost menacing because much more felicious

---

31. *Morne* means "dreary, dull".

than she ever would be able for, and so she mustn't grumble at its insubstantiality. He said "feliss ..." and "insubstant ..."; and she said that long words must be felicity for him—he wasn't able for them.

... They weren't liking Ireland. It had seemed probable they wouldn't, yet they took their honeymoon to see. In London it was thought that *now* there was a chance for Irish Home Rule; so it were wise to see the land before it got contended and uninteresting. Felicia had an Irish friend in London, who amid the native ravings showed sometimes a gleam of common-sense. She, vitriolic about English politicians, said that Sinn Fein [sic][32] was at least achieving this—that Ireland would not be "funny" for the British any more. "You'd better go now, if you mean to go at all." But she had warned them that already Ireland was changed; it wouldn't be what they expected, whichever that might be—a screaming farce, a cooing pastoral, or a grim epic. She added, in a moment of the candour which they knew from Shaw and Synge and Birmingham[33] was truly national, that the Irish had a

---

32. Sinn Féin is the Irish republican party founded in 1905 by Arthur Griffith. These and other references to Irish nationalism and the struggle for independence suggest that the story is set before 1919 and, given the couple's continental travels, before the First World War. In her letter of 11 August 1924 to Macgillivray, Mayne expresses her own disappointment about the results of Irish Independence: "I don't know that, in [the] face of the example of Ireland, I can quite say that I hope you will get your Home Rule for Scotland. In Ireland it has been sad and disillusioning in every way. But then, in Ireland, there had been such a too-exalted vision of what would be the result! I fancy that in Scotland you are clearer-headed, and moreover, not so terribly dark and not so terribly Rose of the World-ed as we have been, and we believed it all! I did, at all events; I thought that Ireland would be the pattern of enfranchised nations. If she only had! I don't now speak of the Ulster question—that was always to be expected to turn out as it has done. But of the Southern Irish, and their dissensions—Ah, it has been heart-breaking, and is still.... The end of dreams, it seems like; but perhaps that is too melancholy a future."

33. Of these three authors, whose plays were performed in London in the early twentieth century, George A. Birmingham is less well-known today. Birmingham, the pen name of James Owen Hannay (1865–1950), was an Irish clergyman and prolific novelist; he was involved with the Gaelic League and is associated with the Irish Literary Revival.

different standard of cleanliness from the English.

A different standard—it was more like none at all. At their fishing-hotel in County Galway they had been initiated. They found plates adhering to the table-cloth, and on undoing them, discovered they were glued down by the *débris* of the plate belonging to the meal before, on which they had been stood to "take away." Egg or mustard or marmalade.... Lant and she made faces at each other; then Lant called the waiter and demanded other plates. The waiter looked wistful (some of the people really did) and said: "Sure that's a pity, sir."

"What is a pity?" Lant inquired, hoping for a show of native queerness. The waiter didn't answer, and Felicia said: "He means the stain upon the table-cloth;" but the waiter then looked at her with a sad surprise, and still said nothing. He procured fresh plates, and these were all right underneath. They never found out what was a pity.

The beds were clean and not too hard; the jugs and basins were not startlingly uncared for, though to English notions rather too much left alone; the basins had faint incrustations on their sides, and when Felicia tried Lant's pumice-stone (for tobacco-stains) on hers, the incrustations came off in a sort of powder.

"It's only the action of the water," she said bravely. "Look, it turns into a little gritty dust."

Lant shuddered; but she said that human nature was fantastic, you never came to the end of it. "I quite enjoy this," she said, scrubbing; but she had to repeat, for bearing-up, that it was only the action of the water.... So they could hardly like Ireland.

Recess,[34] where they were, was a lovely little hole in County Galway, famed for salmon-fishing. This was the one hotel; you lived on salmon and turf-smoke. Turf, not peat; no one said peat, and every one looked amused when *they* did. English: that was the tacit comment, they could guess; and it was strange to

---

34. Recess is a village in County Galway.

find, in the torn tragic land, that "English" meant "amusing." Mockery seemed lurking somewhere; it would have been more comfortable to be looked on as the representatives of tyranny, for then they could have shown their graces, how unlike they were to fevered fancies of the conquerors. But against amusement, joined to the renowned good-manners, they felt helpless, not at all like conquerors; and the abdication was enforced, which had not been their plan ... so it was not entirely surprising that they didn't much like Ireland.

"However," said Felicia, "one has always known that it was quite incalculable."

She was trying to like it, for her sense of justice was her strong point. Lant had none, and said that the whole place was a hum ... but he believed there were good carv ... in Gal.... "Span ...," he said. "Let's go there."

Felicia knew that he meant humbug, carvings, Galway, and Spanish, for her friend had told her of the carvings.

The waiter said there was a big horse-fair on Thursday, so they went on Thursday, thinking they would see more "types." They did see these—old men with laughing toothless faces, clad in tail-coats and knee-breeches, with grey stockings and thick buckled shoes, and high hats with clay pipes stuck in them; young men in loose-hung raiment of thin shrunken-looking yellowish flannel, very sinewy and raking, with narrow bright blue eyes and firm wide mouths—not laughing, like the older men's, but angry, stubborn mouths. Lant and Felicia thought these might be Fenians,[35] or whatever modern rebels should be called, for Fenians were no more, they learnt.... The boys wore petticoats of the same yellowish flannel; they didn't seem to mind a bit! The "Aran men" were most remarkable of all, because of their long loping movements in pampooties of undressed cow-hide, all dun-and-

---

35. Fenians was used as an umbrella term for nationalist revolutionaries in the late-nineteenth and early-twentieth centuries who belonged to the Fenian Brotherhood or the Irish Republican Brotherhood.

white and soft, as on the cows' own backs. "They must wear those to get about the rocks, sir—it's on rock they walk in all the islands. 'Tis from that the Aran men have the queer stride." So Mike of Recess had told them. It seemed right to hear these men speak in an unknown tongue. "The most of them have no English," Mike had said.

The women, whether from Aran or not, were striking in their petticoats of scarlet flannel—such a scarlet and such flannel as one had not seen before and would not see again, away from County Galway. The flannel was incredible for woolliness; the petticoats were very full, and swayed in spreading pleats about the ludicrously high-heeled, thick-laced boots, with brass rims to the heels. There was real beauty in the shawls, though, patterned as they were in grey and black and fawn. Felicia had been told that these were heirlooms, worn from age to age. Most of the women had them closely drawn about their heads. Of the famous hooded cloaks there were but few examples. They were wonderful—the lustrous folds, the hoods in which the face was lost, and when you found it, shadowed and mysterious, looked quite beautiful though it was sometimes old or plain. The cloaks were, really, all they had expected.

But it was later in the morning that they saw *the* cloak. They fled the town, so crowded and so smelly, and, shrinking from the comic little beetle-tram that worked along the high-road, went through the Kingdom of the Claddagh[36] to Salt Hill, the seaside suburb. It was there that, having left Salt Hill and launched forth on a country road, they met with such a cloak and such a wearer as made all the rest a figment, and they felt they had seen Ireland at last.

---

36. The Claddagh is an area in Galway city where the River Corrib flows into Galway Bay. It used to be a fishing village with thatched cottages that became a popular tourist attraction during the late nineteenth century. It was famous for the "King of the Claddagh", the honorary title given to the leader of the community, and for the "Claddagh ring" symbolising marriage.

They turned from one sad, sea-blown road into another, and they met her. She was barefoot, but she carried a new pair of the coarse high-heeled boots, to be put on when she got nearer to the town. As the two came abreast of her, she raised her head, the hood slipped back a little; for an instant they stood still, and she looked at them. When after that one look she turned into the road which they had left, they walked on silent, and a trifle vexed, for it was disconcerting to be knocked quite out of time like that.

Felicia first recovered. There was only one thing to be said; she had the moral pluck to say it. "Cathleen-ni-Houlihan:" but she hadn't the pluck to keep from giggling as she said it—or she *had*, for giggling also was the only thing to do.

Lant said "Yes," and in a moment, "Well!" and in another moment, "What?" But none of these was fruitful, and they walked on in another silence. Still in the silence, they soon found that they had turned back towards the town.

"Are we pursuing her?" Felicia blurted out in her especial way that seemed at first all wrong, but mostly proved all right.

"No, not exactly," Lant said, seriously accepting the suggestion. "We're only going back to see it *now*."

Felicia understood him. "Now" they had the key; they'd look at Galway with a fuller understanding. Though they should not again see her, every street would be informed by her.

They went back by the tram, for, like most tourists, they had been a good deal disappointed in the Claddagh. Felicia had been told of the renowned gold wedding-rings with a design of two clasped hands, which dated from the tribal days; and, like the shawls, came down as heirlooms, but were sometimes to be bought from renegades. Her friend had warned her that to find these was not every one's affair. "But I expected to," Felicia sighed. "I thought we should see people standing at the cabin-doors with rings for sale.... I hate the Claddagh. One would never know it was a Kingdom, if one wasn't told."

Lant asked her if she had supposed the King went in perpetual procession on the roads. "You wouldn't know that England was a King ... if you weren't told," he said.

She said she *had* expected him to be there, somewhere, with a crown of some kind of his head. "A harpless one," she said, and that was quite amusing, she considered; but Lant didn't laugh. She asked herself again if he was cross, but as he went on floating words, she thought he couldn't be. "He might as well be, though," she found that she was thinking; and it rather frightened her. But she consoled herself by settling that the walk had tired them both.

Back in the town, they did not see the girl, but there did seem to be a sort of light on it, and for a while they savoured "Ireland," and were remorseful to their English hearts' content. Reaction had to come, though, and it came with food. They lunched at the Railway Hotel: it was appalling. Every one else was "horse" or commercial, and the coffee-room smelt of both. They didn't dare, in spite of the room's designation, to have coffee, so they soon were out again. Felicia thought she would buy something. Though it wasn't the North, and there was no especial reason why they should be good, she decided to buy handkerchiefs.

They went into a straggling, shabby shop that was *the* shop, and the walker (for there was one, to their great surprise)—the walker had a brogue that, as Felicia knew one said, "you could have hung your hat on." The soft, yet to them still (despite the Irish Players) the barbarian accents, were incongruous with "walking," somehow, and Felicia felt she had another item for her list of the right wrongnesses. "Would ye step this way, ma'am, and the young lady will be showing you the handkerchiefs...." They wasted words as well as other things in Ireland!

The handkerchiefs *were* good. Felicia showed her knowledge of the subject by inquiring if they came from Belfast.

"They do not, ma'am; but 'tis all the same—they come from Lisburn."

Lisburn had no meaning for Felicia; she perceived, however, that this was not guile but information, and bought half a dozen at a costly price. The shop had the cash-system of ball-boxes that run round and clatter down; this, like the walker, was incongruous with the brogues, the non-uniform dress of the attendants, and the bare floor which made the place so noisy. Many peasant-girls were buying; one stood beside Felicia. She smelt turfy and she wasn't pretty, but her shawl and petticoat were splendid. Felicia touched the petticoat with a bare finger, furtively; the fluffiness was unbelievable. The girl on the road had had no scarlet petticoat; perhaps the cloaks were not worn with the petticoats?

They certainly ought not to be; no colour should be there but the rich black about the privet-white of such pale cheeks, the soft rose of the mouth, and the grey eyes that brought all clouded lakes you ever saw on April days into your sense.... But Felicia felt that she had had enough of getting drunk upon lake-water, so she took her parcel and her change, and Lant and she went out into the street once more.

They visited the Protestant Church that once had been the Catholic pro-Cathedral. It *had* fine carvings; so had nearly all the houses—now the shops—in the long narrow street. One had to walk with eyes upturned, to see the carvings, and the streets apparently were never cleaned unless by rain. There was an odd helplessness about the dirt—as it were a giving-up of the attempt to combat anything at all but the "ascendancy." The processions had stopped now, but not the groups of little girls. However, they were getting tired and pathetic; if their hair had not been blonde, they might have fitted in.

Felicia plodded on at Lant's tall side, her gaze uplifted to the attics of the crumbling dark high houses that upon the level of the street would often show an open stall for vegetables or cheap fish or fruit.

"Lant, it's like Rome!" she cried out suddenly. "Upon my word, it is. The squalor and the stateliness, and the rank alleys and the raking blackness!"

Lant said: "But where's the Roman col ... , the yellow och ...?"

"Ochre," she exclaimed, this time. "You don't mean yellow oak!"

For *she* was getting cross. She realised that she was bored, and had been all the time. It was no good pretending she liked Ireland, and Lant was quite as bad as she was. The only thing that cheered her was the sense of sharing disappointment. If he hadn't seen her "Rome," which was a flash of genius, he must be even more *assommé*[37] than she was herself. The girl in the cloak had been arresting, literally; but was anything more banal, after all, than to find just what you came to find, in any country? The girl was that—the type you came to Ireland to be *bête* about, like audiences in London, dropping sentimental British tears on Cathleen-ni-Houlihan. Which had been more obnoxious, the English or the Irish at those plays—the English who were maudlin, or the Irish who were so detestably self-conscious, looking out to see if the effects were savoured? That: "I did not," instead of "No," at the end of *Cathleen*, when the boy was asked if he had met the tiresome old woman! "I did not, but I met a young woman" (or whatever it was), "and she was walking like a queen" ... Effective, certainly; you gulped the first time (*she* had not, the second); but what was the good of walking like a queen, when your country was a subject-one, and no matter how obstreperous it made itself, would never be let go?[38]

Felicia stumbled on; *she* wasn't walking like a queen. You couldn't, as an English-woman in this broke Ireland that mocked at you, with its resentful tattered town that was like Rome. She sighed, and bumped up against Lant, on purpose.

Lant took no notice, just mooned on. They might as well be

---

37. *Assommé* means "stunned, knocked out".
38. At the end of *Cathleen ni Houlihan*, the protagonist changes from an old woman into a beautiful young woman. Critics have commented on the stunning effect of this transformation on contemporary audiences, in both Dublin and London (Roche 2015, 27–8).

getting back to salmon and peat-smoke, and plates glued to the tablecloth, she thought....

"Shall we make off?" said Lant, as if he knew what she was thinking.

"Yes, for goodness' sake!" cried she.

"I mean, altogether," Lant went on. "Right out of the daft country."

He had finished "altogether:" he was getting cross! He hated Ireland as much as she did; that was something.

"We'll get off to-morrow," she agreed; and so they did, but not to London, naturally, till October. They went to France, and had a very different sort of day at Carcassonne. Next year they went to Italy, and then to Spain, and then to Sicily; and they were never bored, and Lant saw all her flashes and made love "endlessly," she said—ostensibly a gibe at the unended words, but really she was thinking of an endless love, an endless sense of one another. For that, *au fond*, was what you lived for it; it was "felicity," and she had got it, and *was* able for it!

Three years after the Irish honeymoon, they dined on a June night at Ranelagh, and Felicia sat beside a man who started a good hare. The Happy Day—*the* day, the pearl. You didn't always know it at the time, but you found out, he said.

"But then you don't get all the good of it," Felicia argued.

"And do you mean to tell me," he exclaimed, "that you keep wild illusions about getting all the good of anything?"

"I do," she said; and then he disappointed her by looking at her eyes, and saying that he did perceive the green in them. Her eyes were hazel; she could not forgive him the banality, and talked to him no more about the Happy Day.

But the idea appealed to her, and strolling up their hill together homewards in the starlight, she told Lant, and then began to speculate about their Day.

"Nemi?" said Felicia, for the day at Nemi had been flawless. If it were the Day for Lant, as she was sure it was for her, they *had* perceived it at the time, and there was no green in her eye.

Lant said that Nemi had been good. "Better than Carcassonne or Evreux—yes; and much much better than Toledo. Toledo was too hot. But I think," Lant said, "I think ..." and then went off into a dream, but murmured through the dream, and though she couldn't make out what he said, he floated words and he had slipped his hand into her arm.

"Oh no," said Lant at last, quite audibly. "Not Nemi."

"Which then?" asked Felicia. But it was no matter; any day would do.

"The day in Gal ..." said Lant, and clasped his hand more closely on her arm.

"The day in Galway!" gasped Felicia.

"Yes—that day in Gal ..." he said again, though not as if he'd heard her.

"But I hated it," she muttered, feeling stunned and sick.

Lant didn't hear that either; she was glad of it directly. For he mused aloud.

"I don't know why, and I don't want to. That's *my* Day. It came togeth ... noth ... was left out." He drew her nearer. But she still felt sick. "And did you know it at the time?" she faltered.

"Yes," he said. "Your man was wrong. One always knows it at the time." (But then he never did agree with any one.)

She walked on, with his hand clasped to her heart.

"And Galway was like Rome," Lant mused. "You said it was, and I said: 'Where's the yellow och ...?' But you were right, and no one could have seen it but yourself; it was a flash of your felicious genius," and standing at their door in the dim starlight, he took hold of her, and gave her a great kiss.

The Man of the House (*Blindman*, 1919)

When old Dr. Mount died, and in a few months Mrs. Mount, the three Miss Mounts left Nottingham for London. Their father had advised them to do this when they became "whole orphans," as he said; there would be better opportunities in London. He meant opportunities in their professions. Melicent, the eldest, was a maternity nurse; Thomasine a masseuse; Constance a dispenser. Dr. Mount had insisted that his daughters should learn a trade—not that they would need to live by it, for each would have a little money. But he held that in another sense all men and women needed an occupation to "live by"; and he had made up his mind that none of the girls would marry. He said to Mrs. Mount that Thomasine and Constance talked too much, and Melicent not enough.

"So, either way, men can't get to know them. If Melicent could speak at *all* —" He mused a moment. "That young Brierly.... But he's as dumb as she is, and if possible a little shyer. Affinity may go too far," said Dr. Mount.

Mrs. Mount was "dumb," like Melicent; but Dr. Mount declared she wasn't shy, so he had got to know her. She had never got to know *him*, but that did not matter; one was enough, he said. She looked up when he mentioned "that young Brierly".

"Yes," said Dr. Mount. "He brought her lilies-of-the-valley the other day, and now she has a bunch of artificial ones in her best hat. Didn't you notice? *I* did."

By the time Dr. Mount died, Mr. Brierly had married a girl whom he had got to know, through her talking enough and not too much. Melicent was maternity nurse to their two babies, for Mrs. Brierly had no idea that there had even been the little interlude, and was determined to engage her both times. The Brierlys had no more babies, but Melicent went on seeing a great deal of them and of "her" children.

While they were quite young, the three Miss Mounts had not been glad to learn their trades. They said it was a shame, or Thomasine and Constance did; Melicent said nothing. But as they grew older Thomasine and Constance became interested, and declared that after all it *was* a blessing not to be old maids.

Melicent, who sometimes of course did speak, said once: "Aren't we old maids?"

Thomasine and Constance both cried that indeed they weren't. You weren't old maids when you were business-women.

"At all events," said Constance, "no one *says* you are."

But Thomasine, who was most like their father, saw a little deeper. "That's not it; you really aren't. Old maids are failures; we aren't failures."

"Oh, I see," said Melicent.

They took their house in London in a long, perfectly straight street which at their end preserved a flavour of gentility. The houses in their block had no bay-windows, porticoes, nor red-brick trimmings; they were reticent, not tall for London, with nice first-floor balconies and hall-doors that well repaid attention from the housemaids. Three shallow steps led up to the hall-doors; the areas weren't abysses.

They settled down with Nana, their old nurse, and a new youthful "general". Melicent and Thomasine worked up their connections; Constance found a post at once. They were not young, but neither were they old; their little incomes, added to their earnings, gave them ease of mind in money-matters. Very fond of one another, and successes now at their three trades, each brought into the common stock an everchanging interest which sometimes quite developed—Melicent's particularly. She entered more familiarly the lives of those for whom she worked than Thomasine or Constance could; but all had anecdotes to make diversion for the others and for Nana.

Nana had her meals with them; they sat together in the evenings. Irene, the new importation, wasn't jealous. She would have thought it awful to be mewed up after dinner in the drawing-room; as for meals, she much preferred hers in the kitchen, where she could eat as she liked and read the story in the *Daily Mirror* while she ate. Every one, in short, was happy, occupied, and sensible.

But there had to be a folly somewhere, and for the Miss Mounts and Nana that was Timothy, the cat. He, like Nana, was a bit of the old home, they'd had him thirteen years. He was black, not handsome, of no special breed, although he had a plumy tail. The tail was Orientalism enough for them. "At all events," said Constance, "he can't swallow his fur." He was uncannily clever; he knew every word you said about him; "in another tick he'd speak to you," said Thomasine.

Like all cats, he did precisely as he pleased to the top limit of his powers. The Miss Mounts and Nana asked for nothing better. To claim anything from Timothy would be to make him less than cat. If he wanted to catch mice, he would; they never shut him in the coal-cellar, or withheld his meals to make him hungry. They bought fish for him three times a week; a saucer of milk stood always full in dining-room and kitchen; he drank tea too, and thin bread-and-butter was as much for him as them.

Timothy repaid their devotion. He showed no favouritism; perhaps, they said, he turned a little more to Nana in his illnesses, and the depression of the mating seasons when he saw the real males (for Timothy, as a kitten, had been "attended to") crouch moaning on the garden wall or leap, still moaning, on the females who allured them. The Miss Mounts were clear-eyed in these matters, and they noticed that he did, at such times, turn to Nana—she was always there for him, and they were not. She did not boast; she couldn't but be proud, yet would have been as proud, they knew, in quite another way, if he had taken his poor puzzled head and body to their laps, for Nana loved the three Miss Mounts with all her heart.

Melicent said once, in May, that if she had realised she wouldn't have permitted the early attention to Timothy. That was natural, the other two said; Melicent's profession led her to think more than they did about "That." The only thing that puzzled them was how she *hadn't* realised—when Timothy was a kitten, she was already a maternity nurse. They asked her, and she didn't answer for a moment; then she said: "Well, I'm the eldest."

Next day she observed, when feeding Timothy at dinner-time, that he had never had his chance. "However, we can make it up to *him*, in some ways."

Thomasine and Constance didn't understand. They saw that she was nervous, as she always was in May, but even Constance who was noted for outspokenness, did not ask her what she meant. She never liked to be asked that; she found it difficult enough to say what she did say.

Constance, like Thomasine, talked enormously—Thomasine the faster, but Constance the more lengthily. Nothing stopped her, except her own giggle. She would break off to giggle, but went on again before the other could break in. Thomasine had learnt to speak at the same time, and let the giggle do what it could for her; occasionally Constance noticed, and did stop.

Constance was the youngest, but the plainest. She was low on the ground, like a dachshund; pale, and wore rimless glasses. The blue eyes behind the glasses were well-set and honest.

A cousin, whom they didn't like, said Connie's eyes were honest, all for nothing. It was silly—how could eyes or anything be honest all for nothing?—but it wounded Constance. "Call her clever! *That* isn't clever, at all events," said Constance, and took off her glasses, wiping them with the silk handkerchief she kept expressly for the purpose. The cousin had said too, when Constance first adopted them, that of all futile vanities she thought that rimless glasses were the chief.

"Smart women wear tortoiseshell rims, as dark as possible. Then the glasses are *amusingly* unbecoming. Isn't it clever?"

"All very well for them!" cried Thomasine. "Other people can't afford tortoiseshell."

"Celluloid or horn looks just the same," the cousin said.

"The fashion will soon die, then—always does when cheap imitations begin," retorted Thomasine, who knew quite as much about smart women as the cousin could; and indeed the cousin laughed and said that Thomasine was right. "But I detest the rimless things!"

It was afterwards that she said that about Connie's eyes. Of course it wasn't clever, Melicent agreed. She said so in her timid manner, looking very nice in her grey cloak with the white bonnet, for she had come back from a case, and met the cousin on the doorstep.

"You look like a nun!" the cousin cried, "with your great melancholy eyes and your clear brows. *Mille-Saintes!*"[39] she said.

They hated that joke of the cousin's, who declared that "Melicent" came from the French, when the Miss Mounts all knew—for a very learned friend of Dr. Mount's had told them—that it was straight from the Greek, and meant as sweet as honey.

Melicent had come in smiling; the cousin pretended to be fond of her and she *was* as sweet as honey, and liked every one who liked her. But when Constance told her, she looked angry, and that comforted poor Constance, who said Melicent was like still waters: "you run deep, I mean." Constance didn't mind being plain, if she *was* plain; she knew she spoke freely enough herself, but it was always kind, at all events, sobbed Constance.

The Mounts indeed were kind. They would lend their telephone to neighbours, and ring for neighbours' cats who mewed at the hall-doors. Once, on a moonlit night, Constance came downstairs when she had taken off her skirt and blouse, and was in her dressing-jacket and *flannel* petticoat, with her hair plaited. She heard a mew outside, and opened the hall-door. Their right-hand neighbour's cat was wanting to get in, so Constance rang. Before she could escape, the door was opened by a gentleman in evening-dress.

"Wasn't it awful?" said Constance, who slipped into Thomasine's room to tell her. "When I remembered I was in my flannel petticoat and my red dressing-jacket, and my hair tied with a bit of boot-lace—!"

---

39. *Mille-Saintes* means "thousand saints".

She giggled, and Thomasine said: "*Boot-lace!* Oh, my goodness!"

"I couldn't find a ribbon," Constance said. "At all events, he mayn't have noticed. I only remembered afterwards, the moon was so bright. He thanked me very much, and said 'Come in, puss.' I suppose he didn't know their cat's name is Girlie. Of course he might have thought Girlie would sound queer when I was there alone, if any one had been passing."

She giggled again, but Thomasine was too sleepy to take advantage. Besides, she felt angry with Constance. That soiled red jacket and a flannel petticoat (why had she taken off her moirette one?) and boot-lace in her hair! It was to be hoped he wouldn't recognise her if he saw her in the daytime.

Thomasine was very nearly good-looking. Her back was quite good-looking. Men who saw her passing quickly, sometimes looked again. She had pretty feet and ankles, and she dressed them well; her clothes sat smartly. Her face—a pointed oval with great breadth between the eyes—was like a leaf, now withered. Thomasine *had* to dress, for she massaged so many fashionable women. From them she picked up hints; they talked to their maids, or frocks and hats would arrive and be unpacked, and Thomasine in this way saw the first-fruits of the "Paris openings"—that was what you said. Her stories were the most exciting of the stock; there were Ladies So-and-So in them, often.

Nana always went to bed soon after dinner, and the Miss Mounts read or sewed. Thomasine and Constance liked the sewing best, for they could talk; but when Melicent was tired, as she sometimes was, they got their books. Timothy sat on anybody's lap, and whoever had him took him to the garden the last thing, and waited for him. He came in quickly, having no temptation to stay out. Sometimes, though, he cried as he came in. When Thomasine or Constance took him down, she told the others when he cried. Melicent, they thought, did not. He must have done it with her too, but she said nothing, for some reason. He slept in her room; he could have slept in anybody's, but Melicent had a sofa—he liked that.

They called him the man of the house, and said the hat in the hall-rack was his. Thomasine often apologised to him at breakfast for reading the papers first, but pointed out that she would have no other chance till evenings, while he had the whole day to himself. Timothy listened, blinking his yellow eyes and smiling. He would put out a paw and pat the paper, as if to say he understood, and Thomasine might have it.

She was the social favourite. Everything combined for that—profession, clothes, looks, "quickness": her speciality was quickness. She knew what everybody meant, except sometimes the cousin. Even she could not explain the thing the cousin said to Melicent about her grey-and-white uniform. "So Puritan; and child-beds are so Pagan!"

You expected coarseness from the cousin; but what could she mean by Pagan? The children were always christened. Melicent said so, and the cousin laughed and kissed her. "Oh, *isn't* it Mille-Saintes?" she cried; and Thomasine herself confessed that she was puzzled.

One summer, Thomasine had a delightful invitation for her holiday. Some old friends who had gone to Cornwall asked her there. None of the Miss Mounts had been to Cornwall, which was a nice part, they knew; and the old friends were dear, so Thomasine accepted. She looked well when she went off, in a check coat and a small, dashing hat, and shoes and stockings that surpassed all earlier ones. As she got into the taxi a man passed, and turned to look again. Melicent and Constance, on the steps with Nana and Timothy, thought that she must know him; Constance ran out and asked her, in a whisper. But she said she never had laid eyes on him before. She was blushing a little. "At all events, he'll know you again," said Constance and Thomasine said "Nonsense!"

She drove off then, alert and gay; Timothy kissed a paw to her, and she to him.

Constance soon departed, leaving Melicent at home, for she was out of work. Timothy was with her, in a heavenly mood, rubbing his head, stretching his paws: "Quite a flirtation," said Constance on the steps, more loudly than she should have, but she *was* a madcap sometimes.

She came home that evening to find Melicent in great anxiety. Not about Thomasine, who had wired and had a comfortable journey; but about Timothy. He wouldn't eat, he wouldn't even drink his milk. The one thing he would touch was water. Like most cats, he never cared for water if you poured it out for him; he'd only take it from the bedroom jugs. Melicent had gone into her room, and found him trying, but the jug was nearly empty. So she filled it in the bathroom: "He waited all the time, the clever little man!" Then he had drunk till she thought he would never stop; but not a morsel had he eaten.

He lay on Nana's lap. His ears and nose were hot; his eyes looked heavy. "We must have the vet.," said Constance, and she telephoned that instant. But they had to dine before the vet. arrived.

He said that there was nothing much the matter; he would send some pills. "You know how to give them?" It would be queer, said Constance, if she didn't; at all events, she worked at a chemist's.

"He'll be all right," the vet. said, hurrying off. Late as it was, he was going into the country about a horse.

"A horse, of course!" said Constance.

"They care about nothing but horses. *I* don't believe they understand cats; at all events, they never do them any good."

The pills came, and she gave Timothy the two ordained. He would sleep in Melicent's room as usual, and if Melicent was going to sit up with him, so would Constance.

Nana was crying. "You mustn't cry," they said. "He'll be himself to-morrow."

"No, he won't," said Nana. "And Miss Thomasine at the Land's End[40]—indeed they may well say it."

---

40. Land's End is a headland in western Cornwall; it is the most westerly mainland point of England.

"We'll wire in the morning, if he isn't better," Constance said. "It's a shame it should have happened, when she's only just gone. But we must let her know, at all events, or else she'd never forgive us, if anything happened."

Timothy got worse in the night; they all assembled in Melicent's room, except Irene. In the morning Constance went out, first thing, and wired to Thomasine: "Timothy very ill. Will wire again during day." She telephoned to her chemist—she couldn't come because their cat was ill.

The vet. came again, and said that Timothy was dying.

"Last night you said there was nothing the matter!" Constance cried.

"Cats are deceptive," the vet. answered.

"The pills did him no harm, you know."

"They didn't do him any good, at all events," said Constance.

Melicent said nothing, but looked like a ghost. Nana said she always knew it. They sat in Melicent's room; they hadn't dared to move him. Irene did the room out gently; she was a good girl.

Timothy lay on the sofa, his head between his outstretched paws. His coat had lost its gloss; his eyes were so dilated now that when you saw them, you might think that he was well—they were so bright. But his little heart . . . his little heart was scarcely beating; he moaned pitifully now and then; he didn't seem to know them. Constance was to give him two more pills; they'd ease his going, the vet. said. She did it beautifully, but when it was done, she cried a moment. Timothy had moaned when she disturbed him. "I *had* to, little man," she whispered. "Do you think I would if I could help it?" and she pressed his head against her breast; but Nana said: "I wouldn't do that, Miss Constance; he wants all the air he can get"; so they dared only stroke him very softly.

They sat up there till lunch-time; then went one by one to lunch, and then sat there again, just waiting.

About four o'clock he stretched a little, opening his eyes. They weren't bright now, but glazed and wild. He turned them upon

Nana. All were kneeling close, but it was Nana that he looked at.

"Little man," she said, and smiled at him; but then she cried: "For God's sake, love, be done with it! Oh, I can't bear his eyes."

Melicent and Constance would have like to cover up their eyes too, for Timothy's were so beseeching and so terrified that they could hardly bear them either. But Melicent said: "He'd feel deserted. *You* do, Constance, if you like"; but Constance said she'd do what she could, at all events. So they knelt, smiling through their tears at Timothy, but now Timothy was gazing at the door as if he wished to run away from them, and something else—he even raised himself a little; but he was too weak; he fell back, gazing still, and uttered a faint growl, as when he saw a dog.

"May I never again see a dumb creature die!" sobbed Nana. "I'd sooner watch a dozen men and women."

She moaned as Timothy had moaned at first; but Timothy had done with moaning. There was nothing but a feeble panting now; then once more the eyes closed—he stretched a paw forth blindly.

Melicent took it in both hands and kissed it. She couldn't see him any more, her tears were gathering so thick—the little paw that seemed to beg for love to help him through.... "Thank God!" said Nana's voice in a few moments; and Melicent knew then that he was dead. She trembled; Constance clasped her hand, and Nana put her arm about them both.

Not long afterwards came Thomasine's wire. She would be with them about seven.

"I *knew* she'd come!" Constance exclaimed. "If only she had been in time!"

But Nana said: "Indeed, I'm thankful one of us was spared it."

Melicent went out of the dining-room where they were having tea—the first meal without him. She came back with him in her arms—quite calm at first, but then she broke down dreadfully. None of them had ever seen her cry like that. Constance and Nana took the little body from her arms, and laid it on the table. His black coat was rough and stiff; the white evening-waistcoat he had kept so beautifully looked all poor and soiled. Their tears fell upon the staring coat; they tried to smoothe it, but it wouldn't smoothe. The cold roughness made them think of rabbits and hares in shops; none of them could ever eat a hare or rabbit.

"Ought we to let her see him?" Constance whispered.

Nana said, "Leave him to me."

They hid their faces.

"Now go out, the two of you, and take a breath of air," continued Nana. "Leave the little love to me."

"You'd never have the strength," said Constance.

"Strength? What strength?" cried Nana.

"It'll be a job, the soil's so stiff."

Nana had a queer look in her eyes, but only said: "Come back in half an hour and see." She pushed them gently out and shut the door.

They went to their own rooms; not out. In half an hour they came back to the dining-room. Nana was there, and on the table still was Timothy. But now there was a white cloth on the table—the best afternoon one, with the Irish crochet border. Timothy was laid on it, his head just raised against a pillow. He was on his side, his front paws lightly crossed, his back limbs turned a little, so he was not at full length. The plumy tail showed beautifully, and the coat no longer stared; it glimmered sleek and dark, and the white waistcoat was like snow. You might have thought he was alive.

"Doesn't he look lovely?" Nana said.

"I thought my nice macassar oil would do it. But it was a job."

She seemed consoled by her success, for she was smiling.

"Yes, he looks lovely, Nana," Melicent and Constance said; but into both their minds had crept a fear. He looked just as if he were alive, and Thomasine might think he was.

"I know!" cried Constance, and she hurried out.

Melicent looked after her, then followed her eagerly. Nana soon went too, for she must was her hands. She looked back from the door and said: "I won't be long, my love."

About seven Thomasine arrived. She looked as trim as yesterday, but that she couldn't help, and her white face was anxious. They shook their heads in answer; then got the taxi away quickly, and drew her to the dining-room. She understood at once, for now a white silk scarf of Constance's was tied in a big bow about his neck, and in his front paws lay a little bunch of artificial lilies-of-the-valley, fastened with white satin ribbon; and Thomasine knelt down and hid her face upon the corner of the table.

She couldn't speak for a long time, though she soon raised her head and looked at him. At last she said: "How beautiful he looks!"—and she got up and kissed his head between the ears. They led her away then, and she took off her things and came to dinner, which was in the drawing-room. Irene had made "Nana's pudding," of her own accord, while Nana had been busy. It was not a good attempt, but very nice of her to think of it, they all said kindly.

After dinner—not till then, they had agreed—they told Thomasine about his sudden illness; and on the way to bed, they went into the dining-room again.

"We'll leave a bead of gas for him," said Melicent. "I know cats see in darkness, but—*he* can't."

She covered up her face again, but did not cry this time.

"Yes, a nice bead, at all events," said Constance, with a glance at Thomasine and Nana, who both nodded. Melicent would miss him worse than they, at night.

"That ribbon shows up very handsome on his coat," said Nana.

"And the lilies look so sweet," said Thomasine. "Where did you find them?"

Constance turned to Melicent, but Melicent still had her hands over her face.

"Well, come to bed, my dears," said Nana then.

They looked back from the door. By the faint light they saw the gleam of the white cloth and ribbons, and his waistcoat and the lilies.

"Long ago," said Thomasine, "in Egypt, people used to worship cats."

"At all events," said Constance, on the stairs, "we made him happy."

Melicent, who was in front, turned quickly round. She looked as if she meant to speak, but she turned back again and went into her room without a word, and shut the door.

The Letter on the Floor (*Blindman*, 1919)

"You pay him, darling," Mrs. Devine had said when the cab stopped before the nursing-home; and she took out the little purse that she had used for years and wouldn't give up using, for it came from Ulick, in Australia. It was all to pieces; everything fell out of it and was put back, and then fell out again.

Now, in the waiting-room, a nurse was asking Larminie for Dr. Dorman's last prescription for her mother. "Perhaps it's in her purse?" the woman said, when Larminie confessed she couldn't find it in Mrs. Devine's satchel. There was no paper in the purse, but: "What's that on the ground?" the nurse said, pointing.

Larminie picked up the folded sheet and opened it, not liking to, but what was she to do—the nurse was waiting, rather cross with her for coming in like this, without the very thing she might have known would be first asked for.

"Well?" the nurse said at last, in a dull, patient voice.

"No; that's not it," said Larminie, and looked up at the nurse with eyes that didn't see her. But in a moment she went on. "I'll … shall I go and get a copy from the chemist? They always keep one, don't they? He's quite near;" and she sat down and took her gloves off. "What do you do that for," thought the nurse, "if you are going to the chemist?" Larminie could see her now, and saw her thinking that, still cross.

Just then the doctor—very tall, excitable, and odd, with a lame leg—burst in on them.

"The prescription doesn't matter," he exclaimed. "I shan't require it now. Your mother must be operated on at once," he said to Larminie. "I mean by that, to-morrow morning. Get her ready, nurse," he added.

"Miss Devine can sleep here, I suppose? Your mother wants you to be with her; nothing to prevent, I hope?"

"No, nothing," Larminie replied.

"You may go up; she's asking for you."

Larminie went up. Her mother was in bed, quite comfortable, not in pain; it seldom was exactly pain. For long she had been ill in this way; now at last the doctor had so far consented to the operation she was always asking for as to have ordered her in here to-day—from one hour to another, literally. But at home, he had told Larminie that even now he wasn't sure that he would operate.

"She's tired of the treatment—won't go on with it, she says, whatever happens. If she sticks to that, there's no alternative to operation. The risk's great; but on the other hand, without the treatment she'll go under, and soon too. I'm brutal with you, but it's necessary. So I thought I'd bring her here and temporise. She'll go back to treatment in the meantime—that's my calculation. An expensive subterfuge, but I see nothing else for it."

Now it seemed as if he had resolved to operate at once. Larminie was well versed in his oddity; he was as skilful as he was eccentric, but one never knew how long he'd stick to anything he said. And here, all over the place as he was, she couldn't get a word with him; she'd have to go on in the dark, until the operation either did or did not happen.

As she went up the stairs, she put the paper, folded now just as before, back in the purse. She meant to give the purse back to her mother. The paper would fall out again, and some one else might pick it up this time, and open it. Insane to leave it here; but what else could she do, unless she told her mother what had happened? "Or I might destroy it;" that thought came to her. She knew that never in the world, as people say, could she do either. And one thing was gained by giving back the purse and letter. She would free herself of the dread sense that she could read the letter through. She had read only a few words; they stood distinct as print upon the sheet; and those had made her sit down suddenly and peel her gloves off—she had felt so sick. If she should read the rest, she might do something more remarkable; and her mother was to go under the knife to-morrow, if the doctor held to what he said.

When she came in, her mother smiled at her affectionately.

"They tell me they can give you a bed here. You don't mind stopping, darling, for to-night at any rate? It will be a comfort to me; but I hope it won't be too much the reverse for you. *You* brought no nothing!"

"Not a thing," said Larminie. She heard herself with wonder; it was like another person listening to another person. "But I can buy a toothbrush, I dare say, before the shops shut."

"What about a night-dress?"

"I must borrow one of yours."

"Why, you'll be lost in it, you little sylph!" her mother said. "I used to be as 'elegant' as you are," she then added, as she nearly always did to any comment on her daughter's slenderness.

Larminie never knew how to answer. She would feel a look come to her face that wasn't the right look; but when one couldn't laugh and couldn't question either Mrs. Devine's word, or the loose corpulence that now, made indolent by illness, she had ceased to "mind"—and she had let herself go terribly, these last few years, in many ways ... poor Larminie was nonplussed, every time she heard that once her mother was a sylph like her.

Mrs. Devine watched her. That was customary too; she seemed to want the look that Larminie could not get right. It pitied, or was sceptical; one wasn't quite sure which, and either was offensive. Yet her mother seemed to want to see.

"Oh yes, my girl, I *was*," she said again. She seemed particularly fond and proud of Larminie at these times, always; and she did to-night, more even than was usual—or perhaps it struck one more?

"How very nice for you!" cried Larminie at last, in desperation. "To be anything like *me* was well worth while." She usually didn't answer, but to-night she felt she must.

"Conceited little thing! But so was I.... What will they give to eat, I wonder? And I hear that dinner is at this unearthly hour—just half-past six, my watch says."

"Yes, it's imminent; and I foresee cold mutton with carbolic sauce.... No! now I come to think of it, I saw boiled chicken and rice-pudding coming through baize-doors. Not bad; though there *will* be the sauce, for it's in everything."

A bell rang; the nurse came in and said that Miss Devine had better go to dinner if she liked it hot. Hers would be in the waiting-room. The nurse was not cross now, but kind and cheerful; Larminie could see that Mrs. Devine liked her, and there wouldn't perhaps be time for her to take the usual dislike, before the nursing-home was done with. That was one thing which had made life difficult of late. Larminie, returning to her Irish home, had found it in full swing—the procession of young women in blue cotton, sometimes competent and sometimes not, but always, always tedious, who now passed perpetually through the friendly though impoverished Devine establishment, where nurses had to be like members of the household, eating, sitting (when they weren't in close attendance, and they often weren't) with the Devines, and talking of two subjects only, operations, and their love-affairs with students or with doctors. It was not much wonder that they palled upon her mother; but though half the time she didn't really need a nurse, Mrs. Devine *would* have one; and this meant a scene every few months or so, and a new girl ("all cap and apron," as the doctor said) who was as much loved at the beginning as detested at the end. Larminie, the elder daughter, had to work it all; the line of nurses seemed sometimes to stretch out to the crack of doom.

This was the "crack," she told herself, alone with chicken and rice-pudding and carbolic sauce in the close waiting-room where she had taken up the sheet of paper, opened it, and read those phrases, beautifully written in the curious hand which looked as if there were a line drawn under every word, so decorous and calm and legible they followed one another. Mrs. Devine's hand—that one admired yet saw, sometimes, with such a craven terror, when she wrote to one and slipped the letters under doors at night; and Larminie or Vanda heard the little sound, and saw the letter lying there, and shuddered.

So it had lain, just now; and the nurse waiting crossly. But this wasn't, even yet, the time to think about it. Larminie must see her mother settled, borrow the night-dress, wish her good sleep, embrace her ... and she knew how lingering a clasp would hold her, how profound a look would urge her answering look. Already, often, she had marvelled at those urgent eyes—*had* she, until to-night?

Before she came to dinner, she had given the purse back. Her mother took it without flinching. Had she forgotten what was in it? She slipped it underneath her pillow with a smile for its unsafeness.

"Everything all right? No pennies dropping on the floor—the silver *is* quite safe, in the one pocket that still has a clasp!"

"Yes. Everything's all right," said Larminie. "The papers too, I think."

She had to say it; but it brought no alteration to her mother's face. Did she forget? and would that make what she forgot much worse, or not so bad?

In bed, all ceremonies over, with her mother's night-dress vastly wrapping her against the sheets that were carbolic like the sauce, the moment came when Larminie might think of it. Three months ago, the thing which caused it came to pass—her own breakdown. They found her lying somewhere, with her eyes wide open in a faint. How long had she been there? No one would ever know.

At first (they told her afterwards) they thought that she was dead.

"I might have been," she said absurdly to her sister, who had always "known."

The others didn't know. But that day, she had told her mother.

Six months before that day she had come home; and after all it had been better. She got away from hoping when she got away from London. Now she could never see him; that was a point gained. Another point was that there were no pigeons. Waking in the morning to the sound of pigeons cooing in the London "garden" ... and she used to listen to them, half-divining how in future spring-times she would hear, and all the leaf and blossom would turn black, and she would lie upon that other bed in the back room behind the dining-room (she had the ground floor), thinking of the day to come. It would be like the others—she was getting used to them—since that on which she learnt from a caretaker at his house that he had gone away a week ago, "for a long time," the woman said. For after many days (much more than seven!) Larminie had plucked up courage, and had crept—it felt like creeping, but perhaps she walked along quite normally—to where he lived, and asked for him, and heard. The woman didn't seem to notice anything; perhaps one hadn't turned so pale, or pale at all. It was extraordinary, what could happen to one without showing.... Not a word; and for—how long?—she had not seen him.

Listening to the birds—the enervation of their soft monotony, the sense of what it signified: a blissful pair together, brooding on their bliss. "*Plaisir d'amour: chagrin d'amour*,"[41] the doves knew nothing of such songs as that. One listened to them, and the tedious tears would come that one was so unutterably tired and ashamed of, for they showed upon one's face, and the tall red-haired servant looked at one contemptuously when she came to take away the breakfast-things. She, and the landlady, both

---

41. Refers to a popular French song, *Plaisir d'amour*, the first two lines of which are: "Plaisir d'amour ne dure qu'un moment // Chagrin d'amour dure toute la vie."

resented such a lodger—never dining out these recent nights, and saving cooking.

Anyhow, she'd have to go. These rooms were too expensive, now she had so little work. Her "post," with its small monthly salary, had gone with him. Money came from home, but home was not so rich that they could send enough to make up the deficiency; unless she could get lots of other work, she'd have to leave not only these good rooms, but London; and he would come back some day. Yet if she did succeed in staying on, and saw him, what was there to do or say? Unless indeed he were light-heartedly prepared to find her here awaiting him, no longer either of the two things she had been to him, but cheerful, reasonable, taking it as all in the day's work? He had said of another girl, left by another man as Larminie was now by him, that "if she'd only had the sense not to play heroine, she might have pulled along quite comfortably till she found another lover." But instead of that (he said) she "engineered a disappearance; no one knew what had become of her."

It was now, as if those sayings had been chosen purposely to ease one off for this. Of course they hadn't been. They were like "protective colouring" in animals; he said them by some sort of instinct. Larminie had shrunk from them; she had not guessed how useful they would be in helping her to see the thing to do, which *was* to disappear, but quietly, not "playing heroine." If she found other rooms and stayed, she need not tell him where she was—that would be disappearing. Far from reasonable, certainly, since all she wanted was to see him; yet she might do that without his seeing her.... His eyes encountering hers, with cold unwelcome looking from them—no, it must not happen. Hers would be glad or else alarmed; and he would hate them either way. One felt forbidden: it was like a mark of shame.

Some day, far in the future, it would make one sick to know that one had ever felt so humble. She foresaw that, with lit, angry eyes that were not *her* eyes yet, for the day hadn't come. But it would come: "the readiness is all;" and in the meantime she went out to look for rooms, so that she need not go away from London.

Looking out for rooms was not so bad. It took up time, at any rate. She could get through the day with credit; then the evening came, and she was caught. It was like playing with the waves at the seaside. Quite big waves didn't catch one; then there came, no matter how one dodged it, the big wave that did. It threw one down; one always went down in the end.... No use to tell herself that she was morbid, that he *would* come back to her, intending everything to go on as before, except the thing which wasn't to, but could be easily eliminated if she had but common-sense—or was it humour? She told herself all that; but something deeper down than even She-under-the-Wave drove on her the assurance that although he might, when he came back and learned that she was here (if she *was* here), come to her gaily—what he expected, counted on, was that she would be gone. He meant this for her as it showed itself to her. Another woman—one with common-sense or humour—might have seen it differently; but he reckoned on her way of seeing it. He didn't want to hurt her; all he wanted was to shirk her. If she could laugh, and go on equably.... She couldn't, and he knew it; so she must go quietly, and not play heroine.

She did find other rooms, much cheaper and as good; she even found some friends with whom she stopped a while; but in the end she had come home. Before she went, he had returned. She heard it by some chance; there was no word from him—how could there be? He did not know where she had gone. But she learnt then how she had hoped that he would write or come to the old rooms. She went there, white with shame, and asked. "No, nobody. No letters," said the red-haired servant, scornfully....

At home, she carefully did not play heroine. The phrase had burnt into her; all her life it would affect her. It was of the things one waits for, as ploughed earth for seed. It fell upon her being, and it made the destined difference. That was what "influence" meant—the seed one was prepared for.... Vanda knew; it was a help, although they hardly ever spoke of it.

Vanda only, till the day—three months ago—when Larminie broke down. The faint; and she had found herself upon her bed, with Vanda and her mother bending over her.

"What is it?" Larminie exclaimed. "What's happened?"

She was dismayed when she learnt what it was; and Vanda had to go away directly—there were visitors. Their eyes met, but Vanda had to go; and Mamma stayed.

"It isn't good for you," said Larminie. "You're always lying down at this hour. I'll be quite all right."

"I couldn't leave you, darling," said Mamma. She looked so tenderly—she could look at one beautifully. One always forgot, then. It had been so from childhood; Vanda and she forgot—they could not help it, though they knew. For it was hard to put away the hope that sprang up every time; they wanted her, and in these moments believed that they could find her. And they thought she wanted them; it was impossible to think that there would come, though there had always come, the other moments when they had to think she hated them. They would forget; and when she looked like this, would tell her things, good things and bad, and she would be what they had dreamed of and were sure that she had dreamed of too. Even though they knew the things would be remembered, and brought up again—how differently!—they still told her; and got frightened afterwards, instead of then.

Just as of old, it happened now for Larminie. She lay beneath her mother's brooding look, and heard herself reveal the thing that only Vanda knew, of all her people. It was "romantic"—no one could have told or heard it without feeling that. The broken words in which it shaped itself were powerless to hide its quality.

"I went there, knowing it would be—that I should be.... He was my lover, and we knew he was to be, before we ever met. It was all understood between us. Everything. We *met* like that, pledged definitely."

Silence then. No need to tell the rest. Her mother knew all that, but had not known that he had been one's lover. She had thought (they all thought, except Vanda) that one "lost one's heart" to him, and that he'd acted rather nobly in departing. Rather cruelly, perhaps, to go so suddenly and silently, but often that way was the best.... She knew that this was in their minds; it wasn't pleasant, but she saw that it was really nothing. There was Vanda to uphold her; and how loyally she'd kept the secret! For their comments had been made to Vanda, and she said that often she had longed to tell the truth, but knew that it was better not. Of course it was; and Larminie was glad she had not told, despite the pang it gave to think that one was looked on as a mere adoring fool, with no response from him. For he *had* loved her. He had tired of her; she had always known he must, but she had thought it would be long enough to "live by, first" as she had said to Vanda, with a little sort of smile that he had taught her. She had been so crude when she went over to him that that sort of smile had not been any use to her, and so she had not learnt it. Life had been simple, before that; even the strange trouble with Mamma was simple, through its violence. There weren't the half-things that you needed a half-smile for. Things like that belonged to London where he "mouldered," as he said; or else to Paris where he "lived," as he said too; and she had never been to Paris, and only then for the first time had lived or mouldered (but it wasn't mouldering for her!) in London. She had been too crude; it could not have gone on; yet ruthlessness was more than need be in the way he left her, all alone, without a word. There would arrive a day (she felt again in some far corner of her being) when she'd see him as he was, and this as it had been; and know that he was less than she could live and think him now. The readiness was all; and she would live and think of him so then, when it could come—the sad strange day, when she would have "got over" it.

... Her mother's eyes were on her, and her mother's arms about her—just as one had used to dream; and there was something in this tenderness that even Vanda's had not given. You were lying on her heart with more than your mere body; you could yield all up; you were not "doing it yourself," so rigorously and unpityingly. Somebody had charge of you. Even with him, it had not been like this. That was not rest—not ever. *He* had said it was, but when he felt it most like rest, it had been least like it, for you. You had felt then much as your mother must feel now: in charge of something. Oh, it was like a dove between your hands, that you must cherish lest it hurt itself—most exquisite, but not like the rest.

... Her mother spoke. "My darling—all that, all alone! How did you do it—how did you get through those days? If I had known, I'd have gone over to you. *Why* did you not tell me?"

"I meant never to tell any one," said Larminie.

Vanda had known, but that must not be told, for Vanda was too young; one oughtn't to have told her, but one couldn't not tell Vanda. And since Larminie's return, they only had said things that had to do with *now*—like that about "enough to live by." Vanda hadn't asked a single question.

"You chose to bear it all alone," her mother said. "You are so brave."

"I didn't choose. I just went on as best I could. Whatever came along.... But I was thinking about him, besides. It wasn't only *my* affair, you see."

Her mother's eyes were bitter now against him.

"I should say he's made it so! I don't think you need shelter *him*."

"No," Larminie replied. "Perhaps I needn't. Well, I haven't. It was a relief—all wrong, though," she said, only half aloud. The sense of rest had been divine; but once her mother spoke, that went; and she felt frightened. She lay, looking out into the room from which she had gone forth to him. It was the same; her mother used to come in here with white blind eyes of anger; or beneath the door, would slip the folded letter. Words would stand there in the ordered writing—all the things you'd told, and how she now regarded them; and things that you had never told, nor ever known that she could think of you—mild little you! But there they were, and you would read them, cringing. *So* it was she thought of you, at night, alone, out driving; or when you went in to see her in the morning, and she sat up in her bed and would not speak to you, with white blind eyes. And you had been great friends, perhaps, the night before!

Fear grew in Larminie. She looked into her mother's face to reassure herself. It bent above her still; it still was wrung with love and pity. But *behind* the face, half-showing in it, waiting for its hour ... was there not something?

Mrs. Devine spoke. "'All wrong?'" (What did she mean? But in a moment you remembered what you'd said.) "Why, darling, don't you trust me? Then I've failed—I've failed. I *have*; I let this happen to my girl. I let her do a thing like this!"

Did she not know that that must vex you? Did she mean it—or was this the way she had of seeing things as other people would, if they were there? It was like acting. Often one had felt that, when she said the other things, so different from this. Were they so different? One shrank from this as one had shrunk from those— the same imprisoned feeling, the same struggling up of something in one, like wings tied. And a sense too of shame, of wanting to hide somewhere, as one did when actors ranted. This was worse than ranting actors, because something in one answered to it. Life was not like that; and yet it could have been, quite easily; one didn't know what made it different. If these things that she said and did were really true—the exits, entrances, set speeches, the effective things to say that *were* effective, but that did not tell the truth—had these been real, you could have played your part in answer. The big scene would get itself enacted, and the curtain would come down. But in reality the curtain never did come down. It was as if something went on long after everybody— audience and actors—had gone home. The theatre was empty, but the curtain wasn't down; and some one lingered on the stage, not acting—huddled up somewhere, afraid and cold, with the dark empty house in front. Something was going on, but not the play.

That was where Mamma was different. It was an endless play for her; the theatre stayed warm and full, and there was always something to be said. Lines, as it were, that came into her part—an endless part she had invented, and would play. Yet she must think these things, else how could she express them? *She* meant them, though they didn't mean themselves. And so her theatre was always warm and lit, and full; there was no cowering creature hidden in the dark. One lay looking at her, and her face was tender still. She had her arms about one, but the sense of rest was gone. She seemed to feel that it was gone. She raised herself.

"I must take better care of you in future, little one. So given to enthusiasms—that's the beauty of you; but it doesn't do, unless you're guarded. I must do the guarding! I've avoided being an old dragon, but I see...."

She looked at you, quite lovingly, while she said that. *Could* she not know? You shut your eyes. You had not meant it for a sign that you were tired, but she took it so.

"You'd like a little sleep. I'll go and lie down too, although I don't think *I* shall sleep!" (You saw the exclamation mark, as if it were in print. He hated exclamation marks; he said the sense ought to supply them.)

"Oh, do sleep!" you cried out, and laughed a little; *you* had said an exclamation mark. "Do sleep, Mamma. It's all gone by. I'll very soon be sensible again. Do sleep." She kissed you, and went out.

The letter to your father, telling him, which you had opened, thinking it was the prescription.... If it had been *kind*! It could have been; she could have told him kindly.

"If anything should happen to me, I consider you should know the type of woman that your eldest daughter is. I cannot say I was surprised, although a more disgraceful story I have never heard.... Quite shameless.... Keep a sharp look-out on her, as I shall while I live.... Her influence on Vanda ... absolutely without shame...."

You said that you'd go out and ask the chemist; then you took your gloves off and the nurse stared at you; then the doctor came and you went up.

Thin, you had felt—thin, crisp, like paper... paper. Very meagre, light, as if you walked on air. Quiet; such a little voice you spoke with. That was all right; she was ill, she wouldn't notice. Then you gave the purse back. Your hand didn't shake; you watched it. She said that about the pennies and the silver; "and the papers," you said. She lay smiling at you, lovingly.

... Some years ago you had gone in to her, a letter in your hand, and said: "I think I ought to tell you that I don't intend to read these any more." You held her letter out, unopened. She was angry. She exclaimed that there were things she couldn't say; if you declined to read these letters, she would not be able to endure you in the house. But she did take the letter back; and you felt guilty as she took it—to do that was horrible for her; you blushed. She saw, and said that you might well blush; and you went away, still blushing. She was right; you should have managed it some other way—*you* should have written!

She again wrote letters to you, putting on the cover: "I demand that this be read." You opened them and tried. You could not; something had grown up in you that stopped you. When she asked (and that was what she did; the only word she spoke to you for weeks and weeks: "May I inquire if you have read my letter? I shall not speak to you again")—when she asked that, you said: "I tried, and couldn't. It's as if you flayed me. Don't write any more, Mamma!" She turned away with a harsh laugh, and did not speak to you again; but still she wrote the letters and put that outside. She hadn't written about this, to you; but perhaps she would some day, and you would open it and see that it was this, and sit there on your bed's edge, trembling.

She enjoyed to write the letters. One could understand that. They were vivid, pages upon pages, going back for years. Not the truth, but *she* believed them. Yes, she must believe them; no one could have "made them up;" and yet not any word of them was true. You never could explain this; Vanda couldn't either.

She was not angry when she wrote them. They were always beautifully legible. She wrote them in her second stage of anger—the cold anger which went on for weeks and weeks. How carefully, in every way, she'd written this one to your father—for in that quick look you'd seen that now and then she had corrected, altering a word to one that said the same thing better. Anything might come in anger—when one wrote along with quivering, weak hand, just blazing down the words upon the paper, hardly to be read, they were so quick and hot. But she had written calmly, choosing—choosing all the words, to write them about you and what you told her, lying in her arms that day.

Larminie, with the carbolic-smelling sheets about her, lay and sought for something to explain it. Something there must be; there always was; but nothing came till the tears came. Still and sharp at first—the little tears that stand within the lids and hurt. But then the softer, big ones came; her heart could lift. The puzzling stopped a moment; she could wait. For this too would be clear some day; nothing was clear while it was happening.

Perhaps Mamma was puzzled too? She might be, every time she did and said these things, not knowing how they came about. Once long ago she had stood near the door and put her hands up on her neck, and said that she was hunted. "I'm a hunted creature." Dreadful it had been—how dreadful! Even now one's heart shrank, thinking of it. Yet at the time, for all the dreadfulness, there had been scorn too in your hearts—those of you who went there. She had felt that, and broken from the room, and cried behind her: "You're vile, all of you—you're vile! You *had* been, all of you; and she had cried it out. She wasn't acting (yet she was) when she fled from the room, as if it were a cage she had found open.... Suddenly, recalling that, you *saw* Mamma—not only then, but always. Life itself was as a cage to her, that she went round and round in like that jackal at the Zoo. The jackal rubbed against the bars, on purpose, every time it turned. Savage and sullen, bruising its poor head—the jackal had to hurt itself, because it was so angry. It was alone; it could hurt nothing but itself; it couldn't hurt the bars. Mamma was not alone; she was surrounded by you all; you were the bars, and she *could* hurt you. Papa, Vanda, Larminie; not Ulick. He had gone out into the world, beyond her cage. That was why he was different for her.

Your very names were part of it. Ulick, Vanda, Larminie: not one of them a family name. To call you by fantastic names had seemed a sort of "getting-out"; then she had found it wasn't—only rubbing up against the bars more gently; and she felt the cage again, and worse because she had pretended for an instant to be out.

She had some other life within her, like the jackal; something that she knew of and had lost, or never had. For animals were born in cages, and yet knew about the other life. And now and then she thought that she could bear it, but she had to shut her eyes for that; and when she opened them again, there were the bars all round her. Anything to hurt them. She was luckier than the jackal, for she could.

Larminie—the one called Larminie—had ceased to be a bar, when she left home. She had got out; for a short time, but still she had got out; and now was back, a bar again. A bar that changed to a free animal, like Ulick; but because she was a woman, it could not be borne from her. Not only "out," but ... all that one had told her. And she had forgotten, in the hearing of the story, that one *was* a bar. It had made pictures for her: broken child, sustaining mother; penitence, confession—all this had contented her a while. But the stage-side of her was like the theatre: she "went" to it. The cage-side was the enduring, hidden side; she lived in that, she couldn't "go to" it; it was herself. She had to be it, wondering what it was. When she went out, that day one told her, she remembered what she had been listening to; the bars grew up again. Most likely, very soon she wrote the letter, put it in the little crazy purse, and then forgot it.

One part of her cared for you—the stage-side. Mother, daughter; it was like a play: she sat and looked at it, and liked it. The cage-side.... She didn't know that that was why she had to hurt you, as the jackal had to hurt itself. "Part of herself:" that only made it worse, because she didn't want that part—it was a bar.

The hideous room was not so hideous in the morning, for the sun came in. Larminie got up. She went to see her mother; they embraced. Her mother had slept well.

"And you—how did you sleep?"

"Much better than I thought I should," said Larminie.

"I'm not to have my breakfast!" Mrs. Devine said. "That's what they mean by 'preparation,' the nurse tells me." But she laughed; it was exciting her. The centre of the stage....

Then Dr. Dorman still did mean to operate? At what o'clock, thought Larminie; and as she thought it, she thought too that soon her father would come in. The purse was under Mrs. Devine's pillow, sticking out a little.

Larminie went down to breakfast in the waiting-room. She had finished before Dr. Dorman came. He saw her mother; then came down and said:

"No: I shan't operate. I've had a talk with her; she'll stay here and submit again to treatment. I pointed out that she had no real right to run such risk, for all your sakes. You'd better go up now; she's asking for you."

Her mother said, when Larminie came in: "Well, darling, he's the same mad clever thing he always was. He says he won't, because I am such a valuable person! So you'll all have to put up with all the fuss for ever and a day. I'm to stop here a while, though, for he wants to have me 'under observation.' I feel just like something at the Zoo!" She smiled at Larminie. "But you must come in every day and look at me. Then I shan't mind my cage so much.... I always turn to you, child—don't I?"

And it was true. She always turned to Larminie.... Theatre and cage—perhaps life was the same for every one.

The nurse came in to "do" the bed. The pillow would be pulled away to shake; the little purse would fall, perhaps. No use thinking of it, since one couldn't say: "Mamma—that letter in your purse...."

Larminie went to her room and put her hat and coat on; she was going home to tell them that the operation wouldn't be. As she passed by her mother's room on her way down, the door was open, and she saw the nurse pick up the pillow. Her mother said: "Give me the little purse. I have some papers in it—are you sure there's nothing on the floor?"

The Peacocks (*Nine of Hearts*, 1923)

On the coverlet were peacocks red and white. It was a Persian pattern, and Alicia wasn't sure—but hoped she knew that peacocks come from Persia, and "belong" so intimately in its patterns that their colour needn't be attended to. Shaking the folds, as she had learned to do expertly like a housemaid so that the coverlet lay straight almost at once, she thought of her blue peacock long ago in Ireland, that knew the hour of tea and never failed to call beneath the window for his cake. He used to come with the resilient step, the public-character's indulgence for the public that a private peacock wastes on his little world. Alicia pictured to herself the groups that in a city park hang spellbound on the paling, hopeful of the last indulgence—when the glittering, rustling feathers shall uplift, and he shall royally pace back and forward in the sun of their delight.

On the minute square lawn that lay beneath the river-window of the Irish drawing-room, how she had loved to watch the magic of that blue and green! It had been like possessing countless jewels. For the peacock was her own, and by his own election. When her father bought him there had been no giving of him; so when he gave himself Alicia was inordinately proud. And she believed that her blue bird could really love her, for he came to her at hours when there was nothing going in the way of food.

Like every joy, this brought its own anxiety along with it. When Mr. Doune had bought the peacock his two daughters had been puzzled and surprised. He must have known as well as they knew how improbable it was that Mrs. Doune would cast off superstition *there* when she would cast it off nowhere. Bad luck from peacocks—sternest article of faith for those who live by omens! But at first she took him quietly, and the two girls had laughed with one another:

"Can she have forgotten?"

"Never—but perhaps she doesn't mind the special sort! 'No wedding in the household.' That's the bad luck of peacocks. Does she *want* us to get married?"

There they had touched upon a mystery—the mystery of their lives. If she did want them to get married, she took strange means to achieve that end. So far as girls can be shut up, she shut them up. They frequently escaped—indeed, their whole lives meant escaping in some sort—but energy would fail them often. Youth and "looks" would prove unequal to such constant effort, and the girls had phases when they quite resigned themselves (and amiably, without resentment) to a mode of life which, as a very plain Miss Quirk had said, when they were met by her on one of the long walks that they would take together at such times: "will turn you into scarecrows like myself." The warning chilled their blood; though, as Alicia said: "She's quite a dear to be distressed—she must be kind." But still, to such a consummation girls could not look forward eagerly; and the encounter with Miss Quirk had put a speedy end to that especial period of tranquillity.

Men came to the house—came often and came variously. "It isn't that," the girls would say. It was that when the men did come, and come again, *they* never knew the price Alicia and Doreen paid for their visits. And the visits hitherto had not been worth that price—could not have been, unless for a grand passion. It was even worse with women. Girls or matrons, women never came without a bankruptcy—a price that no one in the world could go on paying. The two girls declared themselves insolvent for their own sex. Any friendships that they had in it were almost clandestine, liable to destruction every day that dawned—by a note, sent without a word to them, forbidding Miss or Mrs. So-and-So the house. Sometimes the friend, outraged yet loyal, let them know; sometimes, more outraged or less loyal, merely cut them. Mortal flesh and blood was powerless to struggle against this. Only one thing could have availed them—money. But they had only small "allowances"; they could not run away, could not do anything but find a means to bear it. And the means they found was tears and laughter, talks, and the walks so dreadfully summed-up by plain Miss Quirk.

Then, with the peacock's coming, their dark problem took a lighter turn. If he did mean no marriage in the household, *and* if she did not want them to get married—might she not let him stay?

Alicia did not dare to let her heart go all the way. When, in the mornings, she caught sight of him in the "big field" before the house, where bluebells made *his* blue look like some visitant's from fabled caves, investigating heaven tumbled down to upper earth; when, on the garden paths, he challenged purple pansies that refused to be intimidated by his brilliance, or where red roses climbed, gave and accepted brighter hues of glory ... when she beheld him thus, Alicia's heart ached with a prescient pang. For now that he was hers—and it was all too plain that hers he was—how could there be a hope....

"*You* give him cake to-day, Doreen. I'll pretend not to hear him."

"Yes—there'd be just a chance if we could make her think he isn't yours."

For so things were. Doreen must suffer with Alicia; but Doreen, without Alicia, might not at all have had to suffer. This was so fixed that they had ceased to puzzle over it; each had accepted once for all the closer bond it drew between them. "She": how did *she* regard that bond? Neither could guess. They moved as in a land unlit by sun or moon or star when they essayed to penetrate that mind.

So Doreen would crumble cake and throw it to the peacock, who, despite his choice, could not be thought to find the morsel less acceptable. He stuck, however, to his choice in other ways; it was Alicia whom he ran to, walked with, spread his tail for now and then, as if to say: "See what you've won—the heart of him who thus irradiates the earth." And she would stretch her hand and he would come, the dazzling tail still high, and put the princely little head into her hand that quivered with delight. But this, like all the other joys of friendship, was clandestine; and Alicia glanced behind her nervously and moved away from him, if "she" were seen arriving.

Not that their mother, openly, was terrible at all. Coming along the path and seeing this, she would not frown; nothing could be more pleasant than the comment she would make. But the girls long had learnt that this meant only what perhaps was worst of all for them. This was the struggle with herself which she had never won, would never win. They pitied her, but had to pity themselves more. It was no use, she'd never win. Their hopes had died; yet none the less they joined her in the contest—laughing with her, taking as a boon the respite that they knew was only respite; worth its while, for all that ... and indeed the hopes were yet alive, since every time they agonised afresh when struggle ceased, and they, like her, confessed defeat.

Alicia, clutching in her fear at something, clutched at humour. "After all, I mustn't be a fool if she won't let him stay, I'll think about his voice and not about his colour." Sometimes he screened, when she was thus provisionally false—searching, she might have thought, her heart to find if she were true. And she *was* true. Unblushingly she said: "There's something splendid—wild and strange. You feel as if you'd lost yourself on Persian wastes." ... But still she said that when he went (if he did go), she would be sensible about his voice—she would admit that it was raucous.

"Not yet, Camaralzaman.⁴² But *then*!"

One day she came home from shopping just in time for tea. Tea came; and when he didn't, she supposed he had got shut into the garden—went (clandestinely) to look. He wasn't there: he wasn't anywhere about the place. She came back to the house, and at the door she found the housemaid, taking in a parcel.

"Where can the peacock be? I have been looking for him everywhere."

"But sure he's gone, miss."

"*Gone!* What do you mean? He isn't dead?"

"No, miss; but sent away."

"Oh, Annie, what do you mean?" Without a word ... without a single word! She had not dreamed of this, but she knew well what Annie meant.

"The mistress.... Sure I was sure you knew, miss. Cook and I were both surprised when you weren't back to lunch, to say goodbye to him. After you went to town the mistress told me he was going, and the cart came for him just when lunch was on the table."

"I was to lunch in town. The mistress knew.... Where is he gone—who sent the cart?"

"The Governor of the gaol, miss."

In her throat she felt the ache contend with something. There was something funny somewhere. But she couldn't find it now. The Governor of the gaol; and there were green lawns at the gaol, and they were greener, smoother, bigger. He'd be happy in *his* gaol. She couldn't find the thing that made it funny, but Doreen and she would find it—they must find it; and Alicia stood, with Annie's round blue eyes upon her, thinking of Doreen and how they'd find it, and the ache within her throat got quite beyond

---

42. Camaralzaman is the name of a prince in one of the stories from *A Thousand and One Nights*, "The Adventures of Prince Camaralzaman and the Princess Badoura". It reinforces the sense that the peacock in this story stands for the love or the lover Alicia is denied by her jealous and overbearing mother.

control. She couldn't speak, she only bent her head against the pain; her shoulders drew together.

"I suppose the mistress was afraid you'd fret miss, if she told you."

Not to Annie might she answer that! Alicia went upstairs. She went into the drawing-room. Words were upon her lips. She met her mother's eyes; and as she met them felt her own eyes speak, not anger, but the very things she wanted most to hide—her grief and her reproach. She did not say a word. She went to the wide window where her peacock used to call, and stood there dumb. But how she wished that she could speak—break out into the bitter anger that she felt! Alicia knew that if she spoke the tears would come so fast that it would make her mother rise and seek to comfort her. It always was like that. Once she had made you cry, she would be kind. It would be blessed so to cry, but then to feel the treacherous hands console her—and Alicia knew what words would come from her own lips: "It isn't only this—it isn't only this."

... Words she had never said, that seemed to wait the moment of some touch within her, deeper than ever peacock sounded.

She stood silent, seeing without another glance just how her mother looked. That moment when their eyes had met, Alicia saw it—as it were a breaking of the structure, all her mother's face *undone*; and the blue hawk-like eyes afraid. Afraid of what? Something that she could feel in one; something one didn't wish to make her feel, and didn't wish to feel oneself. The way one read her, as we read a book we cannot understand. All this about the peacock: superstition and the struggle; then, as he showed whom he liked best, the yielding ... not to superstition. That was but the pretext. Was it to jealousy—not that one should be loved, but that one loved?

How could that be—she often seemed to hate one. Yet Alicia, in her dim young-girlish vision, now and then saw answers such as this leap forth like flames from some dark, sullen fire—and she fled from them, she would not read them. These were such answers as to harbour must destroy all sense of right in her defiance, make her the prey of that which darted luridly from thwarted forces, seeking out the vulnerable point in her perception, reaching it in moments of Alicia's longing for tranquillity at any price—but then again was swept from contact with her by the wind of her unresting flight. She fled, she rode, upon the will to be herself which, if it broke beneath her, would with her lie blasted in the path of that fierce flame.

This came not often. Even Doreen knew nothing of it. Now, as Alicia stood and gazed out on the empty lawn, her anger and her bitterness had taken full possession; *now*, if she had turned round, her eyes would not have played her false as when she entered. Knowing the look upon her mother's face, she lashed a scornful hatred for its childishness. Yes, like an evil-natured child that played malicious tricks behind one's back!

The Governor of the gaol.... Doreen and she would find the thing that made him funny, but Alicia did not want to find it now. One day they had spoken of his peacocks, wondering what he would think of theirs; and Mrs. Doune had said: "I never knew he kept them."

"Oh, he does more—he breeds them," said her husband. "He goes in for them on business lines."

And evidently she had written to him—saying not a word to any of them, settling it all without a sign....

Her mother's voice came sharply from the room behind Alicia. "Have you been told about the peacock?"

Instantly Alicia turned. She went across the room to where her mother sat. She did not speak; she only stood and looked at her.

"Oh, I was sorry," said her mother. "But you know how I disliked his being here. There isn't only you to be considered. *You* may be resigned to live and die unmarried, but your younger sister's not like you—in any way, I'm glad to say. Don't stand there glowering at me! I am not a bit ashamed of what I've done—you needn't think it." And she looked up in Alicia's face, and suddenly began to cry. Alicia watched her cry a moment; then she went from the room without a word.

How many years ago! Yet still the anger could revive. The tears had never come, nor the wild cry: "It isn't only this...."

If that had come? But pride had been too strong. Now it could never come. Her mother had been dead for years and years. Alicia lived alone with Mr. Doune; Doreen had married long ago.

Between the shaking-out and smoothing of the coverlet, all this! A scene within a scene, and which more actual? As in some lapse of time and space, she had been there in the old Irish room where from the window you looked out upon the broad fair river and the green lawn where her blue bird used to follow her—and she was here in the new-old room of their London house, making her bed before she went downstairs to breakfast with her father. Smoothing out the coverlet, Alicia thought: "If she had lived, how many of my peacocks would have gone! It would have been no use to let her send them all away, nothing was ever any use. Besides ... I couldn't."

Now the bed was smooth as cream. All over it the peacocks, red and white, romantically slender (as the blue peacock had not been!), perched and spread wide their tails. The ash-tree near her window, shaking out its plumes, was like a feathered song made visible. "And ash-trees are unlucky, too! It would have been cut down—some day when I was ... lunching out." A quick thought came and went: "And *have* I been 'unlucky'? Have I cared always for the things that bring ill-fortune? Well, it has been my own life, anyhow."

The peacocks on the bed; the ash-tree by the window; in the drawing-room her Chinese print—again a peacock. All would have been "sent away." And she herself—there would have been no she herself by this time. Lonely for Doreen, she never could have struggled on. What would she have become? "A scarecrow like myself": the words came back to her.

"I keep my peacocks now, myself among them. I'm a peacock." Suddenly Alicia laughed aloud. "My blue bird didn't care about Doreen—he knew his kind!" And she went down to breakfast laughing (bad luck if you laugh before your breakfast); yet within her was the old, reluctant wish—that never could have been indulged, because she was a peacock—for the tears and the wild cry, and the herself that could have let them come.[43]

The Picnic (*Inner Circle*, 1925)

The picnic was for the grown-up Miss Crichton. This was her sixteenth birthday, and she had chosen a picnic on the Old Head[44] instead of a birthday dinner. Rosamund Maryon, who admired her fervently, thought now that she must be even nicer than she looked. Her hair was golden, and she was always laughing. Her name was Persis. Rosamund's mamma said it sounded like something to put in a salad, but Rosamund couldn't help thinking it was lovely.

The birthday cake was there for the picnic, but of course without any candles. "They wouldn't stay lit in the open air. I think it looks just as nice without them." Although Miss Crichton said it, Rosamund couldn't agree with that. Sixteen candles would have been splendid—even her own seven, on her last birthday, had been. But if the cake hadn't been at the picnic, Rosamund and the other children wouldn't have seen it at all.

Mr. Crichton said: "And who knows if there mightn't be another cake at home?"

"That's a shame, to tell on the child," said Mrs. Crichton; and

---

43. This slightly ungrammatical phrase "the herself" in the last line seems to refer to Alicia's "real" self and desire, buried underneath social conditioning and restraint. Since the story was probably written around the time Mayne translated several of Freud's essays (cf. supra), it could be taken to refer to Freud's opposition between ego and id. I am grateful to Catherine Isolde Eisner for this suggestion.
44. The Old Head is a peninsula near Kinsale, where Mayne spent part of her childhood. That the story is partly autobiographical is confirmed by a reference in Mayne's letters (cf. supra).

Miss Crichton got very red. Rosamund couldn't understand why, and asked mamma in a whisper. Mamma said it took away some of the credit. Rosamund didn't understand that either.

After lunch the grown-up people said they'd rest, and Miss Crichton took the children to explore and pick flowers. There were Rosamund and her younger sister Lottie, and two other little girls; no boys. Miss Crichton had no sisters or brothers; she was an only child. (The word "only" sounded quite different, like that, from all the other times you said it.) The children went off with her, and soon they were out of sight of the others.

The Old Head was across the harbour from Kinsale. It was the great place for picnics. When you were coming to it, it didn't look a bit the same as it did when you had landed. The shore was rocky, and there was only one thing growing on it—a little dark-green feathery bush that Mamma said was fennel. It had a queer, rather nice smell. It looked very lonely, all by itself on the shore. One day, when Mamma had taken Rosamund and Lottie to the Head, a storm came on; and when they were getting into the boat to go home after the storm was over, the fennel was being blown about by the wind. It looked as if they weren't there at all, and Rosamund felt a little afraid of it; she didn't know why. She never told this to anyone, though.

But when you went away from the shore and across the grass that wasn't bright green but a sort of yellow green and then into a rocky narrow lane, and then through a gap in the hedge, you came to the lovely part of the Head. You couldn't see the sea any more unless you climbed up; and there were real green fields and lots of little lanes; and to-day (Miss Crichton's birthday, the tenth of July), the hedges were full of honeysuckle and wild roses, and the fields of tall white daisies.

Miss Crichton said they'd better not begin to pick their flowers yet. The roses fell so quickly, and it would be fun to explore a little first. The children obeyed, but it was difficult. Such heaps of roses and honeysuckle! Would they come back the same way?

Even if they didn't, Miss Crichton said, there'd be just as many in the other lanes.

Rosamund saw a blue flower growing high upon a grassy hedge. It was the only blue she had seen, and this seemed to make it unlikely that there would be the same sort in the other places. She would just pick that one, Miss Crichton wouldn't mind, she was sure.

She scrambled up the bank. Scrambling about was what you always did at picnics; that wasn't being disobedient. The flower was entangled with the rose-briars and the honeysuckle; when she came down, possessing it, she found the little lane quite empty. The others must have gone through the gap where once there had been a gate, for you could see the place for the hinges on one side. But when she passed the gap there was no sign of anyone.

The field before her now was bare and flat, with short thin grass. There was a ruined cottage in the middle. The cottage had no roof, and tall weeds grew right up to where the windows had been. There was something about it that frightened her. It looked as if it did not want her to be there. She turned away with a swift backward glance. It was as if an angry person was telling her to go.

The house was only angry till you went away: and Rosamund, no longer feeling frightened, ran down the lane—they must be at the other end of it. There the lane stopped without really stopping in a little field where there were lots of the tall daisies, but no people. That feeling came again, as if her heart was farther in; and now there was no house to run away from. She stood still. She would be sure to find them in a moment. One part of her said that, but another part said: "They've forgotten you. You *must* be frightened," and that part said it louder than the other.

She ran across the field and climbed the hedge at the far end. A wider field was all she saw, and there was no one in it. Rose-briars caught her hair, and they seemed angry. Earth fell down behind her and seemed angry too. All the things looked different—the near ones angry, and the far-away ones, like the bush of fennel that day, as if there was no one there. The roses and honeysuckle were waving in the soft little wind the same as they had before, but now they didn't look as if they were playing. It all looked different—not really farther away, but you felt as if it was.

She got down from the hedge and ran back across the field to the lane. The lane looked different too, but at its other end the gap was, with the little house. They might have been behind the little house! She began to feel sure they were and that she'd see them the moment she got there. But when she reached that end of the lane there was no gap, but a stile instead, and past the stile a rocky shore and heaps of dark brown seaweed and the sea.

The sea was as blue as it had been in the morning when they rowed over in the three boats from Kinsale; but its blueness seemed to be all for itself, instead of being for people to look at, as it had in the morning. The sea looked very proud; and there was something about its proudness that frightened her more than anything else had.

Everything seemed to be saying a word to her—a word that, when she read it in a story, was exciting. When a little girl got lost in a story you weren't sorry for her, because you knew it was going to be exciting to see if they found her. But now, when all these things on the Old Head were saying it, and it was you yourself that was lost, it felt like the stories that made you cry.

She stood on the stile, her hands clasped tight together with the blue flower in them. Her face—they sometimes called her Solemn-Face at home—was very solemn now. She wasn't crying yet—a quiver of the lip at moments, a quick lifting breath.... When picnic-parties weren't on the Old Head there was nobody on it. Nobody had lived there for ages and ages. To-day there were nearly all the grown-up people she knew, and Papa and Mamma, and Lottie, and the other children. But if they couldn't find her they would have to go home without her. Papa would send a policeman to look for her again in the morning; but where would she be by that time? There might be wild animals on the Head in the dark; or there might be mad old men that lived in the holes on the hill, like Old Jacky at Kinsale. Old Jacky lived in one on the hill at Kinsale, near Scilly.

She turned and looked at the bush-covered slopes behind her. The Old Head was watching her. It was saying to itself: "That little girl is lost." But it didn't care; it was only just *thinking* it; and the Old Head was so big that she was afraid when it seemed to be watching her.

If a mad man came now—if Old Jacky came.... He might have come over in one of the fishermen's boats that they had met in the morning, going back to Kinsale; but *he* might have stayed behind on the Head. Constable Egan called him the Wild Man of the Woods, and there was a wood on the other side of the Head. Rosie had often seen Old Jacky lying in his cave upon the hill near Scilly, and once she had met him in Kinsale, on the steps to Compass Hill. He had a long grey beard, all tangled like her hair when it had been washed; and his hair was tangled too, and longer than her own or Lottie's. He ran when he walked—a funny kind of run that wasn't really a bit quicker than walking. Sometimes he ran in this way after little girls; but Bridget said he'd never do a ha'porth of harm to them, poor man! It was only because he was fond of children, and especially little girls. "But let you not be frightened, my pets. I'll take good care he'll never touch you."

But supposing he came now and took her away with him to the cave! Nobody would know, and she would have to live with him for ever and ever.

She stood there at the stile, and tried to think what she would do if they went home without her. She'd have to find some place to hide in. But if she did, they mightn't find her even in the morning. She turned again, ran up the lane again. But this must be another different one, for now a stony path began that she had never seen before, and it was rocky at the sides instead of bushy. Till now her tears—for they had slowly come—had been the silent tears of anguish. Now, on the stony path that hurt her feet, a whimper broke from her; soon the sobs were shaken out by her wild running; but she tried, still running, to consider what she must do next. She'd *have* to hide; and she must look for a cave like Old Jacky's with bushes in front of it. But when could she begin to look, for first she must try again to find the others, and she mightn't find them at all, and how would she know when to stop looking for them and look for a hole instead?

The stony path was very long; she could not see the end of it. As she ran on, she suddenly remembered God. If God would help her, she'd be sure to find them. But He must have seen her all the time, and He wasn't helping her. Perhaps He always wanted you to *ask* Him? But how could she kneel down—if she knelt down, Old Jacky might come behind her. The lane was getting narrower and stonier; dark shadows were coming over the sky. Most likely by this time, especially if it was going to rain, they had gone home; and anyhow they would be going soon, so as not to be late for dinner.

There was no sound at all. If she stood quiet like the other things, it would feel as if everything had stopped and the night would come quicker. She ran on. The path looked just as long, though she had run so far. At last she did stand still. She lifted up her face and said out loud, not kneeling down: "God! Can't you help me?"—not like praying, but as if she was calling to a person like Bridget. The moment she said it there was a soft, near, rustling sound, and something touched her shoulder.

She covered up her head with both her arms. It was God, and He was angry with her for speaking to Him like that.

The sound stopped, and the touch was gone. When she looked up again there was a big white bird in the sky, low down. She knew then that it must have been the bird, not God; but now she couldn't stop being frightened. She did not dare to scream. A scream would make God angry, she was sure. Even Bridget got angry when you screamed. With a moan that wouldn't stop when once it had begun, and that had begun all by itself, she rushed up the stony bank and clung to it, climbing. There were gritty little bushes here and there; she grasped at them, lost hold, slipped down again and hurt herself. The moan went on, but not because she had hurt herself. She mustn't show she minded, or the things would prevent her more, for now she could not doubt that they all hated her for being there. The blue flower was withered, but she held it tight in her hand. It was like something of her own that didn't hate her. It was clutching at the bushes with her, as if it wanted her to get to the top.

Now she slipped down a long way, grazing one arm and shin. For an instant she lay quiet, with her face against the sticking-out white stones. She would have liked to stay like that for ages, and not try any more. She was tired, and her shin and arm were hurting. It would be nice to go to sleep, even like this.

Were they all talking and laughing, just as if she was there—going home in the boats, perhaps home already? Lottie would be in bed, if they were; Bridget would bring her bread-and-milk up to her, and they'd wonder what poor Rosie was doing on the Old Head.

The anguish of these thoughts revived her energy. If she got to the top and didn't see them, she would ... she would ... Tears were streaming now, for now if she didn't see them she would have to begin looking for a cave to hide in. Perhaps, if there was no one at the top, she would scream—but then a mad man like Old Jacky, or Old Jacky himself, might hear her and come running and looking at her, and talking to himself the way he did that day on Compass Hill.

She looked up again at the quarry's jagged edge. The bush that stuck out there must be quite near the top, for she could see a rim of grass above it. Now she reached the bush, caught it, pushed past, and saw the roses and the honeysuckle wave again beyond a little gap. In the gap something stirred. She saw an arm push through the honeysuckle. Her heart stopped beating—she was sure it was Old Jacky. Now someone stood there, looking at her below. It was Miss Crichton, and she was laughing.

"Why, we began to think you must be lost!" Miss Crichton caught her arm and pulled her up, still laughing. She began to beat the chalky dust off Rosie's frock. "What on earth made you climb the quarry, child? The path leads straight to this field. What a state you're in! I hope your papa and mamma won't be angry. Where *have* you been?"

"I don't know," Rosie said, when she could speak. Miss Crichton did not seem to notice that she had been crying; and it made her feel as if she might begin to cry again, though she was found at last.

"But didn't you see us? We must have been quite close—it's only a few minutes since I missed you. Lottie said you'd climbed on a hedge. Well, come along. It's time to go—they've packed up."

She followed to the middle of the field, where on a grassy bank they all were sitting, laughing and eating sweets. The sweets were little round pink ones, called comfits. She never heard the word again, through all her life, without remembering.

No one was angry, but they said that Persis Crichton had been worried at losing her for a few minutes.

"What were you doing, child? She knew you couldn't be far off. Where were you?"

A few minutes. They all said it. They must know how long it was. She could not speak. They had been laughing all the time and eating comfits. It wasn't really unkind of them, for she hadn't been really lost, but she couldn't help feeling as if it was.

"Why, you've been crying!" said Mamma, looking at her more closely. "Were you frightened—did you think we had forgotten you?"

"Poor little mite," said Mrs. Crichton. "It was only a few minutes, or I'd scold Miss Percy well, even if it is her birthday."

"I did cry," Rosie said at last, in a low humble voice. "I thought it was such ages."

Her eyes filled again.

"Poor little mite," said Mrs. Crichton again, and Mamma put

her arm round Rosie's waist; but they were laughing all the time.

"Well, don't cry any more, you know," Mamma said. "That's being silly. You might have known we wouldn't let you be lost."

She took another comfit and put one in Rosie's mouth.

How difficult it was to understand! How could a thing happen to you, and not really happen?

"It was the *same* as if I had been lost," thought Rosie, and she looked at the blue flower in her hand. It knew. It could remember the way they had run up and down, and the bird in the sky, and the time she hurt her arm and leg. No one had noticed the cut on her leg; it wasn't hurting much now, and she hoped they wouldn't notice it, for she ought not to have climbed the quarry. She looked up to the smiling faces round her, and she felt as if she had been ever so far away, in a place they didn't know about at all—not the Old Head, but like a place in a story.

"Well, Solemn-Face? When are you going to look a little more cheerful?"

Mamma said that, and they all stared at Rosie. How could you help looking solemn? It made you feel solemn when you had seen the way things looked when you were lost. People might laugh, but most likely they wouldn't if they had seen too. She would never be able to tell them. It all went away when she tried to think how she would tell them. They said she hadn't been lost; but she must have been, or how could she know the way things looked when you were?

The little pink sweet was melting in her mouth. It had no taste. She didn't like it—not because it had no taste, but because the little sweets *themselves* made her want to spit her one out. There was something horrid about them. They were Mamma's, for she had been handing them round when Miss Crichton said: "Here's the wandering sheep." That was out of the hymn: "I was a wandering sheep, I did not love the fold." Mrs. Crichton said: "Hush, Percy!" but she laughed. Mamma was handing round the sweets and didn't hear Miss Crichton saying that.

Now they were collecting the rugs and baskets, and the gentlemen were getting the boats ready. The picnic was nearly over and she wasn't a bit sorry. It had been lovely at first, but now it was all spoilt. On account of being lost, she had picked no flowers except the blue one. The others had picked heaps. Nobody noticed that she had only one. She felt as if she was by herself inside.

Her blue flower was quite withered, but she could not throw it away when it had been lost as much as she had. She must keep it until she could put it in water. Then of course Lottie would notice it was the only one she had, but she could say: "At all events, it's the only blue one we found." It might look as blue as it had at first when it had had some water. Flowers often didn't look as nice till they revived, as Mamma said.

Going home, she was in the bow of the boat with Lottie and one of the others. She didn't say a word more about having been lost, and they didn't either. Some of the sea was golden and dancing, and the boat went right into the golden part. It was lovely; and a lot of the feeling of having been lost went away. If only it didn't come back when she woke up in the night! Sometimes things did, like the day when Old Jacky ran after them on Compass Hill. Bridget said he wasn't running after them. That was the same as their saying she hadn't been lost. How could you feel as if a thing had happened when it hadn't?

When she was landing at Kinsale, the blue flower fell into the sea. She was dreadfully sorry for a moment, but then she forgot, because she was to carry one of the baskets. They said good-night to everybody, and Miss Crichton kissed them all and said they had given her a lovely birthday. She didn't say anything different to Rosie—she said to all the children: "Don't forget to put your flowers in water before you go to bed. Now promise!" They all promised. But how could Rosie promise? She knew her face got very red, but no one noticed; and Miss Crichton never noticed either that she hadn't promised.

Bibliography

Primary Sources

<u>Novels</u>
1902. *Jessie Vandeleur* (London: George Allen)
1908. *The Fourth Ship* (London: Chapman & Hall)
1913. *Gold Lace: A Study of Girlhood* (London: Chapman & Hall)
1916. *One of Our Grandmothers* (London: Chapman & Hall)

<u>Collections of Short Stories</u>
1898. *The Clearer Vision* (London: Unwin)
1910. *Things That No One Tells* (London: Chapman & Hall)
1917. *Come In* (London: Chapman & Hall)
1919. *Blindman* (London: Chapman & Hall)
1923. *Nine of Hearts* (London: Constable; New York: Harcourt, Brace)
1925. *Inner Circle* (London: Constable; New York: Harcourt, Brace)

<u>Biography and Criticism</u>
1909. *Enchanters of Men* (London: Methuen; Philadelphia: Jacobs)
1910. *The Romance of Monaco and Its Rulers* (London: Hutchinson; New York: John Lane)
1912. *Byron*, 2 volumes (London: Methuen; New York: Scribners)

1913. *Browning's Heroines* (London: Chatto & Windus; New York: Pott)

1924. *Byron*, revised edition, one volume (London: Methuen; New York: Scribners)

1929. *The Life and Letters of Anne Isabella, Lady Noel Byron: From Unpublished Papers in the Possession of the Late Ralph, Earl of Lovelace* (London: Constable; New York: Scribners)

1939. *A Regency Chapter: Lady Bessborough and Her Friendships* (London & New York: Macmillan)

Short Stories

[Frances E. Huntley]. 1895. "A Mercenary Girl", in *Hearth and Home*, 8: 205 (18 April), 845.

[Frances E. Huntley]. 1895. "A Pen-and-Ink Effect", in *The Yellow Book*, 6 (July), 286–91.

[Frances E. Huntley]. 1895. "Her Story and His", in *Chapman's Magazine*, 2 (November), 286–92.

[Frances E. Huntley]. 1896. "Two Stories", in *The Yellow Book*, 8 (January), 47–64.

[Frances E. Huntley]. 1896. "His Glittering Hour", in *Chapman's Magazine*, 3 (April), 439–48.

[Frances E. Huntley]. 1897. "Unto the Shore of Nothing", in *Chapman's Magazine*, 7 (May), 34–9.

1907. "The Invitation to the Valse", in *The Pall Mall Magazine*, 40: 176 (December), 644–52.

1909. "Your New Hat", in *The Pall Mall Magazine*, 43:189 (January), 72–7.

1910. "Dispossession", in *The Nation*, 7:18 (30 July), 630–31.

1910. "Four Dances", in *The Nation*, 7: 24 (10 September), 834–36.

1911. "Atherley", in *The Nation*, 8:16 (14 January), 643–44.

1911. "As a Lamb…", in *The Pall Mall Magazine,* 47:214 (February), 209–12.

1912. "The Colonel", in *The Pall Mall Magazine*, 49:229 (May), 679–85.
1912. "Vanity", in *Vanity Fair*, 3 July, 15.
1913. "Reassurance", in *The Nation*, 13:9 (31 May), 342–43.
1919. "The Man of the House", in *Land and Water*, 74: 2979 (12 June), 17–19.
1922. "Stripes", in *The Golden Hind*, 1:1 (October), 31–4.
1923. "Black Magic", in *The Westminster Gazette*, (March), 9.
1923. "The Shirt of Nessus", in *The Golden Hind* 2:5 (October), 15–20.
1923. "The Turret-Room", in *31 Stories by Thirty and One Authors*, ed. by Ernest Rhys and C.A. Dawson Scott (New York: Appleton), pp. 182–203.
1923. "Lovells Meeting", in *Georgian Stories 1922*, ed. by Arthur Waugh (London: Chapman & Hall; New York: G.P. Putnam's Sons), pp. 230–44.
1923. "Stripes", in *The Best British Short Stories of 1923*, ed. by Edward J. O'Brien and John Cournos (Boston: Small), pp. 208–15.
1923. "The Turret-Room", in *31 Stories by Thirty-and-one Authors*, ed. by Ernest Rhys and C.A. Dawson Scott (New York: Appleton), pp. 182–203.
1924. "Dialogue in a Cab", in *The Transatlantic Review*, 1:2 (February), 41–45.
1924. "The Difference", in *The Transatlantic Review*, 1:5 (May), 318–20.
1924. "Humour", in *The Golden Hind*, 2:4 (July), 19–20.
1926. "The Lower Road", in *Atalanta's Garland: Being the Book of the Edinburgh University Women's Union* (Edinburgh: Edinburgh University Press), pp. 33–51.
1927. "The Picnic", in *Georgian Stories 1926*, ed. by Arthur Waugh (London: Chapman & Hall; New York: G.P. Putnam's Sons), pp. 169–80.
1928. "The Lower Road", in *Georgian Stories 1927*, ed. by

Arthur Waugh (London: Chapman & Hall; New York: G.P. Putnam's Sons), pp. 242–57.

1928. "The Separate Room", in *Great Short Stories of Detection, Mystery and Horror*, ed. by Dorothy L. Sayers (London: Gollancz), pp. 1201–29.

1929. "The Separate Room", in *The Omnibus of Crime*, ed. by Dorothy L. Sayers (New York: Harcourt, Brace), pp. 1150–77.

1930. "Ugliness", in *The New Statesman*, (27 September), 761–2.

1931. "Ugliness", in *The Best British Short Stories of 1931*, ed. by Edward J. O'Brien (New York: Dodd, Mead), pp. 136–141.

1932. "The Man of the House", in *Puss in Books: A Collection of Stories about Cats*, ed. by Elizabeth Drew and Michael Joseph (London: Geoffrey Bles), pp. 188–202.

1934. "Light", in *International Short Stories*, ed. by Virginia Church [Woodson Frame] (New York: Lyons & Carnahan), pp. 276–312.

1935. "A Bit of Her", in *Life and Letters*, 11:63 (March), 692–96.

1936. "The Man of the House", in *The Faber Book of Modern Short Stories*, ed. by Elizabeth Bowen (London: Faber), pp. 315–30.

1938. "Stripes", in *An Anthology of Modern Short Stories*, ed. by J. W. Marriott (London: Nelson), pp. 65–75.

1950. "The Shirt of Nessus", in *The Uncertain Element: An Anthology of Fantastic Conceptions*, ed. by Kay Dick [Jeremy Scott] (London: Jarrolds), pp. 139–58.

1957. "The Man of the House", in *Great English Short Stories*, ed. by Christopher Isherwood (New York: Dell), pp. 249–65.

1977. "The Separate Room", in *Human and Inhuman Stories*, ed. by Dorothy Sayers (New York: Manor Books), pp. 149–76.

1992. "A Pen-and-Ink Effect" in *Femmes de Siècle. Stories from the '90s: Women Writing at the End of Two Centuries*, ed. by Joan Smith (London: Chatto & Windus), pp. 216–21 [as "Frances E. Huntley"].

2016. "The Separate Room", in *Homefront Horrors: Frights Away from the Front Lines, 1914–1918*, ed. by Jess Nevins (Mineola, N.Y.: Dover Publications), pp. 187–214.

Selected Essays, Reviews, Journalism

1905. "Cork and Queenstown", in *The British Isles, Depicted by Pen and Camera* (London and New York: Cassell), pp. 116–121.

1912. "Two Novels" (Review of Winifred Letts, *The Rough Way* and F.E. Penny, *The Out-Caste*), in *The Nation*, 12 (9 November), 294.

1913. "The Seer Blind" (Review of D.H. Lawrence, *Sons and Lovers*), in *The Nation*, 12 July, 577–78. (Rpt. in *D.H. Lawrence: The Critical Heritage*, ed. by R.P. Draper (London: Routledge and Kegan Paul, 1970), pp. 69–72.

1918. "Henry James (As seen from the 'Yellow Book')", in *The Little Review*, 5:4 (August), 1–4.

1919. "Aroma" (Review of *Little Women* [Theatre Ed.]; Hector Malot, *Nobody's Boy*; E.C. Cowper, *Maids of the Mermaid*; A.M. Irvine, *Maida the Tenderfoot*; Elsie Oxenham, *A Go-Ahead Schoolgirl*), in *The Athenaeum*, 4675 (5 December), 1313–4.

1922. "Women and the Modern Novel", in *The Yorkshire Post*, 6 February, 11.

1922. "Folly Redressed: Some Reflections on Cats", in *The Yorkshire Post*, 29 May, 10.

1923. "Reading the Cards: The Fascination of the Mystic Alphabet", in *The Yorkshire Post*, 25 June, 6.

1923. "The Spell of Proust", in *Marcel Proust, An English*

Tribute, ed. by C. K. Scott Moncrieff (London: Chatto & Windus), pp. 90–95.
1924. [A Tribute to Joseph Conrad], in *The Transatlantic Review*, 2:3 (September), 345–47.
1925. "Introduction", in *The Adventures of a Younger Son*, by Edward John Trelawny (London: Oxford), pp. v-xv.
1928. "Introduction", *A Byron Library: A Catalogue of Printed Books, Manuscripts and Autograph Letters by George Gordon Noel, Baron Byron*, collected by Thomas J. Wise (London: Printed for Private Circulation Only), pp. xxi-xxvii.
1932. "Wild Caro" (Review of Elizabeth Jenkins, *Lady Caroline Lamb*), in *The New Statesman*, 3:69, 801.
1935. "Byron" (Review of Peter Quennell, *Byron: The Years of Fame*), in *The London Mercury*, 33, 70–1.

Poems
1902. "May Day at Sea", in *The Academy and Literature*, 1566 (10 May), 491.
1923. "The Tribute", in *The Golden Hind*, 2:5 (October), 24.

Archival and Other Material
Death certificate for Ethel Colburn Mayne, Newton Abbot Registration District, No. 245, registered 2 May 1941, Torquay, Devon.
Hartnoll, Phyllis. 3 February 1940. "Reader's Report on 'Sentence of Life' by Ethel Colburn Mayne". British Library. Macmillan & Co. Collection, Readers' Reports, Vol. 3769, no. 184.
Mayne, Ethel Colburn. 13 January 1921. Letter to Katharine Dexter McCormick. Private collection of Susan Waterman.
Mayne, Ethel Colburn. 1924–1927. Letters to James Pittendrigh Macgillivray. National Library of Scotland,

Correspondence and Papers of James Pittendrigh Macgillivray, Acc. 3501/6.

Mayne, Ethel Colburn. Letter to Lovat Dickson. The University of Reading, Macmillan & Co. Ltd. Archive, MAC MAY, 196/62.

Secondary Sources

Contemporary Reviews, Essays and Books

Anon. 1898a. "Fiction", in *The Saturday Review*, 86:2243 (22 October), 544–5.

___. 1898b. "Short Stories", in *The Athenaeum*, 3705 (29 October), 606.

___. 1898c. "*The Clearer Vision*, by Ethel Colburn Mayne", in *The Bookman*, 15:87 (December), 87.

___. 1903. "Jessie Vandeleur, by E.C. Mayne", in *The Academy and Literature*, 1601 (10 January), 32.

___. 1908. "*The Fourth Ship*. By Ethel Colburn Mayne", in *The Academy*, 1886 (27 June), 932–3.

___. 1913a. "*Byron*. By Ethel Colburn Mayne", in *The English Review* (January), 323.

___. 1913b. "Browning's Women", in *The Saturday Review of Politics, Literature, Science and Art*, 116:3031 (29 November), 685.

___. 1913c. "*Browning's Heroines*, by Ethel Colburn Mayne", in *The Athenaeum*, 4492 (29 November), 616–7.

___. 1923a. "*Nine of Hearts*, by Ethel Colburn Mayne", in *The Spectator*, 7 April, 22.

___. 1923b. "Advertisements by Harcourt Publishers", in *Daily Mail*, 29 September, 4.

___. 1925. "Inner Circle", in *The English Review* (May), 685.

Bowen, Elizabeth. 1945. "The Short Story in England", in *Britain Today* 109, 11–16. Rep. in Phyllis Lassner. 1991. *Elizabeth Bowen: A Study of the Short Fiction* (New York: Twayne), pp. 138–43.

Douglas, George. 1912. "The New Life of Byron", in *The Bookman*, 43:255 (December), 188–9.

Egerton, George. 1905. *Flies in Amber* (London: Hutchinson)

___. 2006 (1893, 1894). *Keynotes and Discords* (London: Continuum)

___. 1932. "A Keynote to Keynotes", in *Ten Contemporaries: Notes Toward Their Definitive Bibliography*, ed. by John Gawsworth (London: Ernest Benn), pp. 58–60.

Ellis, Havelock. 1896. "Friedrich Nietzsche", in *The Savoy* 2 (April), 79–94.

Harland, Henry. 1897. "Concerning the Short Story", in *The Academy* 1309 (5 June), 6–7.

___. 1896. "Dogs, Cats, Books, and the Average Man", in *The Yellow Book* 10 (July), 11–23.

Hoult, Norah. 2016 (1944). *There Were No Windows* (London: Persephone)

Hueffer [Ford], Ford Madox. 1920. "Thus to Revisit...", in *The English Review* (July), 5–13.

Isherwood, Christopher (ed.). 1957. *Great English Short Stories* (New York: Dell)

James, Henry. 1898. "The Story-Teller at Large: Mr. Henry Harland", in *The Fortnightly Review*, 63:374 (April), 650–654.

Mansfield, Katherine [K.M.] 1920. "Dragonflies", in *The Athenaeum*, 4680 (9 January), 48.

Matthews, Brander. 1994 (1901). "The Philosophy of the Short-Story", reprinted in *The New Short Story Theories*, ed. by Charles E. May (Athens: Ohio University Press), pp. 73–80.

Nietzsche, Friedrich. 1896. *Thus Spake Zarathustra. A Book for All and None*. Trans. by Alexander Tille (London and New York: Macmillan)

Poe, E. A. 1994 (1842). "Review of Twice-Told Tales", reprinted in *The New Short Story Theories*, ed. by Charles E. May

(Athens: Ohio University Press), pp. 59–64.
R.H.C. [A.R. Orage]. 1918a. "Readers and Writers", in *The New Age*, 23:23 (3 October), 365–6.
___. 1918b. "Readers and Writers", in *The New Age*, 23:25 (17 October), 397–8.
___. 1918c. "Readers and Writers", in *The New Age*, 23:27 (31 October), 429.
Swinnerton, Frank. 1913. "Novels in Solution", in *The Bookman*, 45:267 (December), 174–5.
___. 1918. "Three Woman Novelists," in *The Bookman*, 53:317 (February), 158–9.
Wells, H.G. 1992. (1911) "Introduction to *The Country of the Blind, and Other Stories*", reprinted in J.R. Hammond, *H.G. Wells and the Short Story* (Basingstoke: Macmillan), pp. 162–6.
W.W.T. 1909. "Some Royal Mistresses and Courtesans", in *The Academy*, 1944 (7 August), 395–8.

Literary Criticism
Adams, Jad. 2006. "Mayne, Ethelind Frances Colburn", *Oxford Dictionary of National Biography*. https://www.oxforddnb.com/ [Accessed July 20, 2019]
Baldwin, Dean. 2013. *Art and Commerce in the British Short Story, 1880–1950* (London: Pickering & Chatto)
Abu-Manneh, Bashir. 2011. *Fiction of the New Statesman, 1913–1939* (Newark: University of Delaware Press)
Battershill, Claire. 2018. "'Tricks of Aspect and the Varied Gifts of Daylight': Representations of Books and Reading in Interwar Women's Periodicals", in *Women's Periodicals and Print Culture in Britain, 1918–1939. The Interwar Period*, ed. by Catherine Clay et. al. (Edinburgh: Edinburgh University Press), pp. 14–27.
Beauman, Nicola. 2008 (1983). *A Very Great Profession: The Woman's Novel 1914–39* (London: Persephone)

Blondel, Nathalie. 1998. *Mary Butts. Scenes from the Life* (Kingston, New York: McPherson)
Binckes, Faith and Carey Snyder. 2019. "Appendix", in *Women's Periodicals and Print Culture in Britain, 1890s-1920s. The Modernist Period*, ed. By Faith Binckes and Carey Snyder (Edinburgh: Edinburgh University Press), pp. 436–57.
Buchholz, Sabine. 2003. *Narrative Innovationen in der Modernistischen Britischen Short Story* (Trier: Wissenschaftlichen Verlag Trier)
Chan, Winnie. 2007. *The Economy of the Short Story in British Periodicals of the 1890s* (New York: Routledge)
Cleary, Joe (ed.). 2015. *The Cambridge Companion to Irish Modernism* (Cambridge: Cambridge University Press)
D'hoker, Elke and Stephanie Eggermont. 2015. "Fin-de-Siècle Women Writers and the Modern Short Story", in *English Literature in Transition*, 58:3, 291–312.
___. 2016. *Irish Women Writers and the Modern Short Story* (Basingstoke: Palgrave Macmillan)
___. 2017. "Artist Stories of the 1890s: Life, Art, and Sacrifice", in *Reconnecting Aestheticism and Modernism: Continuities, Revisions, Speculations*, ed. by Bénédicte Coste, Catherine Delyfer and Christine Reynier (London: Routledge, 2017), pp. 92–106.
___. 2020. "Daughters, Death and Despair in Ethel Colburn Mayne's Short Stories", in *Irish Women Writers at the Turn of the Twentieth Century*, ed. by Kathryn Laing and Sinéad Mooney (Brighton: Edward Everett Root), pp. 143–54.
___. 2021. (forthcoming). "A Forgotten Irish Modernist: Ethel Colburn Mayne", in *Irish Modernisms: Gaps, Conjectures, Possibilities,* ed. by Paul Fagan, John Greaney, and Tamara Radak (London: Bloomsbury)
Farrell, Marcia. 2007. "Elizabeth Bowen: A Selected Bibliography", in *Modern Fiction Studies,* 53:2, 370–400.
Fluhr, Nicole M. 2001. "Figuring the New Woman: Writers

and Mothers in George Egerton's Early Stories", in *Texas Studies in Literature and Language*, 43:3, 243–66.

Fogarty, Anne. 2002. "Mother-Daughter Relationships in Contemporary Irish Women's Fiction", in *Writing Mothers and Daughters: Renegotiating the Mother in Western European Narratives by Women*, ed. by Adalgisa Giorgio (Oxford: Bergahn), pp. 85–118.

Gasiorek, Andrzej. 2012. "Exiles: *The Transatlantic Review* (1924–5) and *The Exile* (1927–8)", in *The Oxford Critical and Cultural History of Modernist Magazines, Volume II: North America 1894–1960*, ed. by Peter Brooker and Andrew Thacker (Oxford: Oxford University Press), pp. 697–717.

Golding, Alan. 2012. "*The Little Review* (1914–1929)", in *The Oxford Critical and Cultural History of Modernist Magazines. Volume II: North America 1894–1960*, ed. by Peter Brooker and Andrew Thacker (Oxford: Oxford University Press), pp. 61–83.

Goldman, Jane. 2009. "Desmond MacCarthy, *Life and Letters* (1928–35), and Bloomsbury Modernism", in *The Oxford Critical and Cultural History of Modernist Magazines. Volume I: Britain and Ireland 1880–1955*, ed. by Peter Brooker and Andrew Thacker (Oxford: Oxford University Press), pp. 428–451.

Hanson, Clare. 1989. *Short Stories and Short Fictions. 1880–1980* (London: Macmillan)

Havighurst, Alfred F. 1974. *Radical Journalist: H. W. Massingham (1860–1924)* (Cambridge: Cambridge University Press)

Hunter, Adrian. 2007. *The Cambridge Introduction to the Short Story in English* (Cambridge: Cambridge University Press)

Ingman, Heather. 2009. *A History of the Irish Short Story* (Cambridge: Cambridge University Press)

___. 2007. *Twentieth-Century Fiction by Irish Women. Nation and Gender* (Aldershot: Ashgate)

Keown, Edwina and Carol Taaffe (eds). 2010. *Irish Modernism. Origins, Contexts, Publics* (Oxford: Peter Lang)

Kreilkamp, Vera. 1998. *The Anglo-Irish Novel and the Big House* (New York: Syracuse)

Ledger, Sally. 1997. *The New Woman. Fiction and Feminism at the Fin de Siècle* (Manchester: Manchester University Press)

___. 2007. "Wilde Women and The 'Yellow Book': The Sexual Politics of Aestheticism and Decadence", in *English Literature In Transition 1880–1920*, 50:1, 5–26.

Oxford English Dictionary (OED) Online. Oxford University Press. https://www.oed.com [Accessed September 1, 2020]

O'Toole, Tina. 2013. *The Irish New Woman* (London: Palgrave)

Pykett, Lyn. 1992. *The "Improper" Feminine: The Women's Sensation Novel and the New Woman Writing* (London: Routledge)

Roche, Anthony. 2015. *The Irish Dramatic Revival* (London: Bloomsbury)

Rogers, Stephen. 2009. "Nostalgia and Reaction: Austin O. Spare and *Form* (1916–17; 1921–22); the *Golden Hind* (1922–24); and the *Decachord* (1924–31)", in *The Oxford Critical and Cultural History of Modernist Magazines. Volume I: Britain and Ireland 1880–1955,* ed. by Peter Brooker and Andrew Thacker (Oxford: Oxford University Press), pp. 552–570.

Samuels Lasner, Mark. 2006. "Ethel Colburn Mayne's 'Reminiscences of Henry Harland'", in *Bound for the 1890s: Essays on Writing and Publishing in Honor of James G. Nelson*, ed. by Jonathan Allison (High Wycombe, Bucks.: Rivendale), pp. 16–26.

Scholes, Robert. n.d. "General Introduction to The New Age 1907–1922", *Modernist Journals Project.* https://modjourn.org/general-introduction-to-the-new-age-1907-1922-by-scholes-robert/. [Accessed 22 September, 2020].

Waterman, Susan Winslow. 1999. "Ethel Colburn Mayne", in *Late-Victorian and Edwardian British Novelists: Second Series*, ed. by George M. Johnson (Detroit: Gale), pp. 187–201.

Windholz, Anne M. 1996. "The Woman Who Would be Editor: Ella D'Arcy and the *Yellow Book*", in *Victorian Periodicals Review*, 29:2, 116–30.

Also published by *EER*
Now available or coming soon

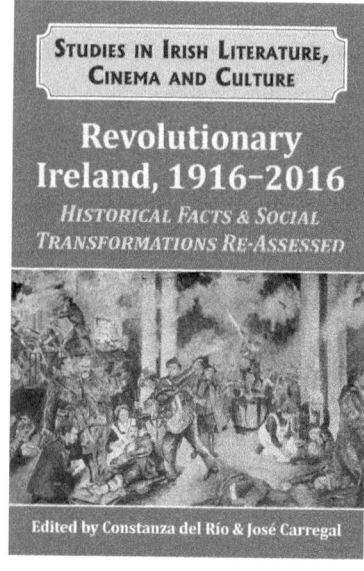

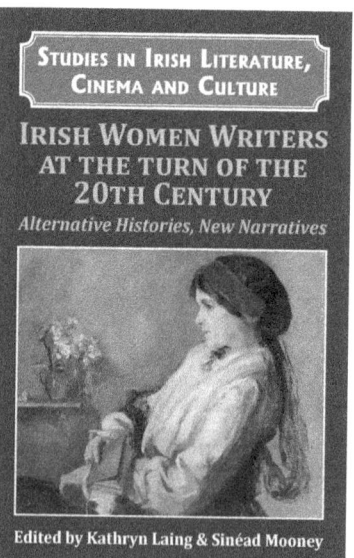

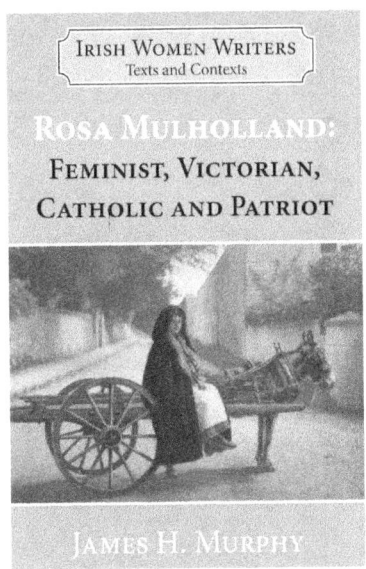

www.ingramcontent.com/pod-product-compliance
Lightning Source LLC
Chambersburg PA
CBHW052043300426
44117CB00012B/1956